- yc
  er

- yc

- yc

- yc

- yc
  cu

- yc
  p

- yc
  b

HERTFORDSHIRE LIBRARY SERVICE

WITHDRAWN FOR SALE

Please renew or return items by the date shown on your receipt

**www.hertsdirect.org/libraries**

| | |
|---|---|
| Renewals and enquiries: | 0300 123 4049 |
| Textphone for hearing or speech impaired | 0300 123 4041 |

Hertfordshire

523 175 65 8

# Testimonials

Antony Welfare provides a holistic account of not only how Social Media has evolved to become THE dominant marketing tool, but also provides key insight into how Social Media can change how business is conducted. This book provides easy-to-understand steps that show how Social Media can increase your market share via intelligent application and careful strategic positioning.

*Chris Davies*
*Managing Director, Engage Insight*

-------

Antony is steeped in sales and passionate about Social Media. This book covers everything from the basic 'What is Social Media?' through to what the future might hold. But the bit in the middle is priceless for any business – how to create your Social Media strategy presented in a straightforward and easy plan to be implemented today. Enjoy!

*Sue Ingram*
*Executive Coach*

-------

People are usually caught in one of two categories; 1. Knowing about Social Media but not understanding why they should get involved; 2. Getting wholeheartedly involved but not getting results – and still wondering why. With this book, it really puts everything into perspective in a clear concise read that can be used to build your strategy. Social Media is here to stay. People are jumping on the bandwagon without a clear understanding of why and therefore not utilising this massive marketing tool – and it's FREE! Antony sets out the why, the when and, quite simply, the how. An essential read for anyone in business.

*Gill Tiney*
*Co-founder of BeCollaboration, international speaker, author and coach*

KV-512-189

As a business owner, I loved Antony Welfare's encouragement to see that your Social Media community is one and the same as your customer base – and that it's now absolutely vital to be part of the E-Revolution. A website alone won't do; we simply must now embrace the global opportunities offered to us via the technology of today AND tomorrow. Do you know your company's keywords? Do you 'get' the power of hashtags? Is your LinkedIn profile working hard for you? If not, you're missing huge tricks. Showing all the advantages and disadvantages for each Social Media channel and how to use them to gain sales, this book equips you, in easy-to-understand terms (no web Klingon required!) to take your business to the level it needs to compete with one and all, just by selling and marketing products using the online Social Media models. It's like gaining a huge online High Street presence without any real estate costs or leaving home! Best of all, it's no matter that our marketing budget cannot compete with the multinationals... because Social Media is free... therefore making your investment in this book the best return ever!!

*Jane Malyon*
*Founder and Director, The English Cream Tea Company*

-------

This book is an excellent Social Media guide for experts and trusted advisers looking to use their book as a marketing tool. I will be recommending it to my clients.

*Richard White*
*Author of 'Consultative Selling for Professional Services: The Essential Sales manual for consultants and other trusted advisers'*

-------

This practical, down-to-earth guide is an essential part of any business owner's toolkit. Antony's expertise and passion shines through as he clearly illustrates the importance of Social Media and how it can revolutionise your business. Highly recommended.

*Prue Nichols*
*Author of 'The Natural Laws of Work: How to stay cool, calm and collected in the office'*

3

In today's technologically advanced world where there is so much information and noise, the challenge for many entrepreneurs is how to utilise, harness, and maximise Social Media to communicate their unique message, be heard, engage with their customers, and get their product known to the right customer that is ready to buy. This book is a brilliantly executed, comprehensive Social Media guide for the modern age entrepreneur. Read this book cover to cover and implement all the steps discussed; you will nurture the seeds of your business to grow and become trees that over and over produce fruits.

*Tony J Selimi*
*Bestselling Author, and Elite Life and Business Success Coach*

-------

This book gave me a very clear roadmap of how to not just to set the right goals, but equally important, how to deploy the strategies effectively and efficiently to achieve maximum results. The book shows me that utilising little of my time, Social Media has the ability to explode my business on a global scale with 100% sustainability built into it!

*Tina Allton*
*Co-director of Circle Podiatry. UK's #1 multi-award winning private podiatry brand*

-------

Not only does it guide you beautifully into the right mindset around Social Media, especially if you are a bit averse, but it gives you clear, easy and doable steps to create and action an effective Social Media plan. Highly recommended.

*Jessica McGregor Johnson*
*Life Guide and Mentor - connecting you to your spirit, the true heart of you.*
*Author of 'The Right T-Shirt'*

This book is dedicated to all business owners
who wish to understand what Social Media can do
for their business and their customers.

I would like to thank my family
(A, B, C, K, M and V, C and M)
and all my friends for their
continued love and support.

*"Social Media is a significant enabler
to increasing your business success
for little investment,
but with a high return."*

Antony Welfare

# About Antony Welfare

Antony is an experienced Retailer, E-commerce, Digital and Finance Consultant. Antony spent 15 years with international retailers, before moving into smaller multi-channel and pure e-commerce retailers.

Antony is the author of the international bestseller *The Retail Handbook* and the creator of the UK-wide Digital High Street Skills programme. Both the book and the training programme are aimed at helping smaller businesses learn from the larger retailers and learn how to trade successfully online.

Antony has launched three brand new e-commerce businesses and relaunched two fashion brand e-commerce businesses, as well as developing the Dixons e-commerce businesses from the beginning.

Antony's experience in retail is an impressive list of skills and achievements, including developing the Store of the Future programme for Marks & Spencer, managing the UK e-commerce websites for Dixons Retail and integrating a newly acquired £80m turnover B2B company.

He created a new European Shared Service Centre (SSC) where he developed the business and implemented SAP. After two years, he employed 250 people and serviced 11 countries. He later became Finance Director for the Dixons Commercial team.

Antony established a pure e-commerce business from scratch, launching an entire brand, range, marketing programme in nine months. Following this, Antony has developed a number of multi-channnel and e-commerce businesses, partnering with the existing teams or developing new teams to implement successful businesses.

Antony was born into a family of retailers. In the 1920s, his great grandfather Jack, at the age of 26, set up a very successful provisions shop in Kent.

The shop traded successfully for many years with Jack diversifying into nurseries and garden centres until they were bombed during the war. Jack did not let this stop him and he continued the shop, and it is still trading in Kent to this very day.

Antony's own career started in a newsagent at the age of 15; Antony was soon running the shop on a Saturday and Sunday morning from 6 a.m. until 10 a.m. – no mean feat for a 15-year-old. Managing the morning newspaper delivery team, ensuring all the stock was correct and dealing with the early morning customers before the weekend business started in earnest later in the day. The excitement of dealing with stock and customers led him to give up the usual 'sports Wednesday' at school in preference for some more time in the shop. This is where he dealt with the stock orders and delivery, ensuring the shop was able to function efficiently.

This was when he fell in love with retail, and this progressed throughout his life and still to this day. Once at college, he started work at Sainsbury's as a checkout assistant and soon progressed to helping the customer service team and coordinating the checkout queues.

With retail now firmly in his blood, he went to Loughborough to study Retail Management for four years. Whilst there, he continued to work in Sainsbury's and would often work 30 hours a week, alongside study and a hectic social life.

In 1996, Antony went to Marks and Spencer for his year in industry. This is where he started to learn the real detail of running a successful retail business. Based in the Chester region, Antony experienced the excitement and complication of running an extremely large and successful M&S store. During the year, he was responsible for the Christmas gift shop, learnt the ways of HR and finance, and managed the store in Wrexham for two weeks.

On graduation, he moved to London to start on the Sainsbury's Graduates Programme, spending one year at HQ in the property area and one year in the trading area for Homebase.

He then moved on to Marks and Spencer where he spent five years at HQ, learning the trade in areas such as Store Development (where he developed the Store of the Future programme), Design, Buying and Merchandising, and the Financial Services business. During his time at Marks and Spencer, Antony qualified as a Management Accountant (ACMA)

The following five years were spent at Dixons Retail, where he looked after the UK e-commerce sites, the Dixons chain (now Currys.digital), a newly acquired £80m turnover B2B company and finally spending two years in the Czech Republic creating a new European Shared Service (SSC). The SSC was developed and built from scratch, and after two years it employed 250 people, serviced 11 countries and was finalist in the European Shared Service of the Year Awards. On return from the Czech Republic, Antony was the Finance Director for the Commercial team in the UK.

In 2009, he left Dixons Retail to set up the e-commerce arm of SmartWeave. SmartWeave had been set up eight years previously, to invent the world's only fabric which eliminates sweat patches. The 'SmartWeave' technology is patented in the US and China, and is pending in the UK and Europe.

Over the last few years, Antony has worked with many retailers, entrepreneurs and fashion brands, developing their retail business and growing their online presence and success.

In 2014, Antony created, and rolled out the national training programme to get High Street retailers online and working in the digital world – Digital High Street Skills in association with People 1st and the ATCM.

 antony@retailpotential.com

 @AntonyWelfare

 http://uk.linkedin.com/in/antonywelfare

 facebook.com/AntonyWelfare

# Soci@l Media Essentials

## for a Growing Business

## Antony Welfare

Social Media has come of age - find out what it can do for you.

Published by
Filament Publishing Ltd
16, Croydon Road, Waddon, Croydon,
Surrey, CR0 4PA, United Kingdom
Telephone +44 (0)20 8688 2598
Fax +44 (0)20 7183 7186
info@filamentpublishing.com
www.filamentpublishing.com

© Antony Welfare 2015

The right of Antony Welfare to be identified as the author of this
work has been asserted by him in accordance with the Designs and
Copyright Act 1988.

ISBN 978-1-910125-86-1

Printed by IngramSpark

This book is subject to international copyright and may
not be copied in any way without the prior written
permission of the publishers.

# Contents

# Preface

The world of Social Media has revolutionised our lives. Whether we accept it or not, there is no doubt that Social Media is here and makes an impact on our everyday life.

I absolutely love Social Media and have embraced it wholly. I live my life using Social Media for both business and pleasure. I am a technology and gadget person, and Social Media was new to me in 2007. It took me a while to get into the world of Social Media, mainly due to privacy concerns, but once I fully embraced it, my life changed for the better.

I can say that thanks to Social Media, I have added a lot of value and joy to my personal life and I have added a lot of value to my businesses and my own understanding of life.

The great benefit of Social Media is when you can share and help your community grow and become happier and more informed. This has been the biggest benefit for me and my life. I can now add value to my community in whichever part of the world they live in.

Social Media allows you to see and understand the world like never before, and this should not be taken for granted.

The world of the Internet and Social Media is not without problems, but you can manage your risk by using Social Media intelligently. I have never experienced any big problems with Social Media. It takes time to get used to it and understand it for yourself, but once you do, it will add value.

I hope this book helps you understand more about the world of Social Media, and you learn how to market your business and build a customer community around your business.

I wish you all the best on your Social Media journey, and I look forward to interacting with you on your way.

Very best wishes

Antony Welfare
@AntonyWelfare
antony@retailpotential.com

# Introduction

Welcome to my book, which aims to help you navigate the world of Social Media.

In this book, I will discuss the world of Social Media, and more importantly what it means for your book and your business. I will take you through my tried and tested processes and help you understand which Social Media channel is right for you and your business.

I have lived in the Social Media world for a few years and have experienced amazing connections and life-changing meetings from using Social Media.

Welcome to my book which aims to help you navigate the world of Social Media for your growing business.

In this book, I will discuss the world of Social Media, and more importantly what it means for your business. I will take you through my tried and tested processes and help you understand which Social Media channel is right for you and your business.

I have lived in the Social Media world for a few years and have experienced amazing connections and life-changing meetings from using Social Media.

I have written a book specifically for you as a growing business, to help share my extensive experience over the last few years, growing businesses, in part using Social Media.

As described later in the book, I was born into a retailing family, where my great-grandfather bought and ran a provisions shop opening in 1923.

**H. CHAPMAN**
WILL OPEN
HIS
*New Grocery and*
*Provision Store*
ON
**MONDAY.**
Choice Selection of
Cooked Meats, Dennys Bacon,
Farm Butter.
PERSONAL ATTENTION TO ALL ORDERS

**6. HIGH STREET.**

I spent 15 years in large corporate retailers, and in 2009 I left that all behind and set up a new e-commerce business. This was a new challenge for me and we made a great success of the business, in part via Social Media.

Following this success, I have subsequently launched and re-launched five e-commerce and retail businesses, all of which were highly driven by Social Media. The use of Social Media to grow a business has now become a skill and I advise many companies on e-commerce and using Social Media to grow.

Social Media is still a relatively new form of marketing, and as such, there is much misunderstanding and concern. I have real experience in using Social Media to grow businesses and I share that experience here in the book.

I am learning more and more about Social Media and businesses every day – I know I always will, but I have enough knowledge to share with you some of the models and strategies you need to implement now.

I am a structured person, and as such, you will find a number of models and processes – I make no apologies for this; I am writing this book for you to implement and use some of the ideas and strategies in your own business. They are tried and tested in my businesses and the ones that I advise to my clients.

Not all of the strategies are relevant to every business, but there are enough to help all businesses make a difference and start to use Social Media in a planned and strategic way.

We have always had business plans and marketing plans, so why not have a Social Media plan? You need to plan your Social Media and I show you how to do this in the book.

The world is changing at speed, and we need to ensure our businesses are taking every advantage they can to satisfy and impress their customers.

To put the current world into perspective, I want to introduce The E-Revolution. The E-Revolution has brought about some very big changes to our lives and our business lives. Social Media is one of these changes and we are all trying to work out what this new world is going to do for our businesses.

Along with all the technological changes, the world of Social Media has been born. It started off slowly, but gained traction and is now a major part of our daily lives.

My book is designed to take you through the uses and benefits of Social Media for your business. Social Media can be used for any business, and finding the best way to use Social Media is key for a successful business.

Remember: your customers are using Social Media, your competitors are using Social Media...YOU must use Social Media for your business.

Along with all the technological changes, the world of Social Media has been born. It started off slowly, but gained traction and is now a major part of our daily lives.

My book is designed to take you through the uses and benefits of Social Media for your business. Social Media can be used for any business and finding the best way to use it is key for a successful business.

# Chapter 1: Introduction to Social Media

# Background to Social Media – It is new and it is global

In this book, we look at the exciting and very current world of Social Media. Social Media has been around for a few years, but one thing that people do not realise is that Social Media is such a recent phenomenon, it has really only been active for 10 years or so. The way we use our Social Media accounts on our smartphones, you would think we have all grown up with Social Media.

So what is Social Media?

---

**My definition of Social Media:**
**The interaction of people and communities**
**via electronic methods**

---

We look at Social Media as the various websites, apps and businesses that allow people to connect with each other around the world. Communication and connecting is not a new phenomenon, but to do this electronically with people around the world is where we have a new opportunity and an exciting future ahead of us.

The wide adoption of Social Media by large proportions of the population, and in being used for businesses, has only really been made possible with the improvements in technology; computing devices and of course the speed of the Internet. We now have wireless access to the Internet via our smartphones and tablets – this has only been available in the last five to ten years.

I would argue the widespread adoption of Social Media is only really the last five years or so, even though Facebook (one of the clear leaders in Social Media) is 10 years old. At the start, Facebook was not anywhere near as big as it is now – it started small and has grown to over one billion users, and is still growing.

Just sit back and think about that one fact... on Facebook, YOU can connect with one billion people across the whole world...When have you ever had the opportunity to do this before?

If you look at Facebook, then follow some of the other Social Media giants, such as Twitter, LinkedIn etc., they have only been used for businesses for the last five years. It is fair to say that Social Media is a new phenomenon, and it has grown much quicker in the last two years, even in just the last year.

It is important, at the outset, to understand this growth and the sheer fact that Social Media is now incredibly important for business. In my view, if you are not present on Social Media, you are not present in the world as it stands today.

Everybody uses Social Media, it is everywhere – the access to Social Media channels is now so much bigger than it was, and that is really why Social Media seems as though it has been around for a while, but it has not.

The other fascinating element of Social Media is that it is a global network. You are linking with people in every continent, in most countries around the entire globe! Social Media is global, it is everywhere – as long as you have got an Internet connection, even if it is a slow Internet connection, you can connect.

Being connected is one of the biggest benefits of Social Media – you can connect with people you have never even physically seen, or speak to people in places you would never even dream of visiting.

Social Media gives you the ability to connect and talk, chat, share ideas, share images, share videos and most importantly, and what businesses should be doing – share knowledge.

You can share knowledge with people in any corner of the world, as long as you have got some sort of Internet connection and some sort of connected device. You can learn new knowledge from people in every corner of the world and see images from every part of the world. Social Media opens up the world for you and your business.

Initially Social Media was a local method of communication, but businesses have woken up to the power of what Social Media can do for your business in the commercial context.

*So, Social Media is; New, Global and Connected –*
*it is the biggest change in the E-Revolution so far*
*and it will only get bigger and better.*

As I mentioned in the start of the book, you must approach Social Media, and this book, with an open mindset. In the book, I will discuss the fears people have with Social Media, and I share my own personal story about how I fought Social Media until I needed to use it. That period of my life changed my world, and Social Media was a big part of this positive change.

As we start the book, please open your mind and believe me when I say that Social Media is easy to use and fun... trust me, you will love using Social Media and it will enrich your life forever.

## The history of Social Media

There are many views on how Social Media started. In this book, I discuss what I know from my extensive real-life experience, and share the journey that I have seen and been a part of.

Facebook is the start of real Social Media – there were social networks before, but I do not believe these made a big difference to the world, whereas Facebook has led the way and become the biggest network so far.

Social Media started as a local communication method, namely "The Facebook" which was shortened to Facebook quite quickly after it was launched. Facebook was invented for people on a university campus to chat. That was the main goal of Facebook; to chat, share images, tell people where they were going and what fun they were going to have.

This was in 2004, and what has happened since then is that businesses have worked out that Social Media is one of the biggest new forms of "getting messages out there" – getting business understanding out there and making commercial transactions happen, like never before.

Social Media has grown significantly in terms of the business possibilities, with the likes of Facebook, Google and Twitter, who are all gearing up for businesses. They want to help businesses communicate messages, whether it's a small business, a microbusiness or a multi-billion pound international business, they are all starting to use Social Media, but because Social Media is new, people are still finding their way through this new world.

As a business owner, you are at the start of this journey for your business, and you should have comfort in the fact that nobody really knows how Social Media works across all businesses, and we are all learning this new world.

In this book, I explore the different Social Media channels and discuss what they are used for. Armed with the knowledge I give you in this book, you will be able to start your journey into Social Media, and find what methods and ways work best for you and your business.

All business owners need to get on board the Social Media train...now; it is only going to grow further and it is only going to get bigger. The more people that join Facebook, the more people that join Twitter etc., the more possibilities you have to share your message and to share your messages with people around the world.

There are many different ways you can use Social Media and they are evolving and will continue to evolve. Learning what they are today will help you understand what will happen as these networks get bigger and better, and allow you to be a part of this world and not be a bystander.

## Social Media is changing the way we do business

Social Media is changing the way we do business; it is changing where we sync into our support networks and our business services. The business world is becoming a very connected and a non-geographic business world. If you use any Social Media channel, within minutes you will find connections around the world – instantly, you can connect with people and businesses like never before.

We all need to appreciate that Social Media is here now, and it allows us to create our own space in the world; our own expertise, and our own communities.

In the past, we have always strived to be known for something, but only really big businesses had the resources and capabilities to be known as the expert in an area that crosses borders. Only big businesses could be known for something globally; they could be experts in something, and to be worldwide, they had to be big.

The new world is much better; you can be one person and you can use your own uniqueness, your own experiences in life, to become an expert and share that message with the world. People want to know why you are unique and they want to listen to you as the expert in your area.

We all have different experiences in our lives, but we all share things in common and being connected, being worldwide, as Social Media allows you to be, is the conduit that allows you to share your message, and share your expertise with the world, which then opens up many business opportunities for you as a business owner.

The business world has adapted to new technologies that have been part of the E-Revolution. All these technologies are allowing us as business owners to become more and more connected. Becoming part of a connected community is what drives and grows us as people and our businesses.

Social Media is the conduit that allows the new technologies of the world to be used in a practical way. For example, sharing videos, which contain messages about your business, can now be uploaded quickly and shared on many different Social Media channels. That video could reach millions of people in a short space of time... How did this happen in the past? Did this ever happen in the past?

In the past, the way to get your message across was to write to people and talk to people face-to-face – this is very time-consuming and allows you to reach a very small proportion of the population.

Today, you can use Social Media to reach millions of people who want to hear about your business. All it takes is an investment of time to learn the process I will talk you through in this book.

## Focus on your customer – Think "customer" from now on

All types of business from consultancies, advisors, retailers, e-commerce, and anything to do with selling to customers, starts with your customer, understanding them and giving them what they want, and then you have to treat them, look after them, and share with them. If you treat a customer well, they will then become part of your community and help grow and expand your message in your business.

You must understand what it is that your customers are looking for. You are not selling them what you think they want; you are selling them what you know they want.

> *Understanding the customer and what they want*
> *is more important than what you think they want.*
> *What you think they want is what you want,*
> *not what they want.*

You must understand the customer from their point of view; interacting with them and asking them the right questions is key to running a successful business.

You can only understand your customer by talking to your customer and interacting with them, and the great thing is that Social Media allows you to have a conversations with your customers, whether they are in your town, or somewhere else in the world.

In fact, you can use Social Media to fine-tune your products and make sure that what you are selling is absolutely what there is a demand for.

Using Social Media to understand what your customer wants gives you the best product ever, because if you produce the product that the customer wants, and via Social Media, you can find out what they want; they will tell you. You can produce the perfect product for your customer.

In the end, you are solving their needs, you are solving their wants, which means they will buy your products, they will buy into what your message is and what your community is, but it all starts from understanding your customer inside out.

I will let you know at this stage, that throughout this book, I use the words "customer" and "community" in the same way. As a retailer, I always think about my customers, but my community is also my customer. Think of them as one and you will find this book of great use.

## Know your customers' habits – Visualise your customers

### *The saying goes,*
### *"A happy customer will tell five people,*
### *whereas an unhappy customer will tell eleven."*

This means that knowing your customer is the only way you can make them happy. How can you make anybody happy if you do not know them?

The great part about getting to know your customer, is that once you have a happy loyal customer, you can guarantee that the people they tell will become loyal new customers. They in turn will deliver more potential customers to you; this will help grow and develop your business and community.

In order to understand your customer, and be able to sell the products and services they want, you really need to understand what makes them buy your products and services. To do this, you need to understand their lifestyle; their likes and dislikes, their daily routines, their hobbies, their holiday destinations, the issues that are important to them, etc.

Ask them, directly or indirectly, what are their interests, sports, hobbies, etc. Use this understanding to model a picture of their lives – look for trends in the information you find out.

To gather the customer information, use the resources you have around you and use your Social Media networks.

Possible ways to find out more about your customers:

1. Your team. Good team members will always interact with your customers, so ask them what they know about your customers' lifestyles. There will be many areas of your customers' lifestyles that they will know already. Help them to collate this information and discuss how it can help your business.

2. Your stakeholders. Around your business, there are many people who want to help you succeed and help sell your products and services. These are the people such as your accountant, your publisher, your marketing partner etc. Ask them what they know and understand about your customer.

3. Hold VIP events to gather data from your customers. Your book launch is a great place to do this. Offer some free drinks, nibbles and a discount in exchange for their time completing a short questionnaire, whilst they interact with you and your team.

4. Send out a questionnaire. Using Social Media, you have great opportunities to ask your customers and potential customers questions. The questionnaire should cover all areas of the customers' lifestyle and be detailed enough to allow you to analyse the results and information.

5. Set up and build up a customer database – a must for all businesses. Collect your customers' email addresses when they purchase an item. When they request a free download, ask for their email address in return.

6. Email a short questionnaire to your customer database. Again, the questionnaire needs to be detailed, user-friendly and take up no more than five minutes of their time.

## Social Media – My story

I wanted to share with you the story about how I have become so passionate about the world of Social Media. It was never the case that I was born and bred with Social Media, or even leading-edge technology.

My life when I was younger was without Internet. I remember black and white televisions at home, and at school we used BBC computers once a month or so. My education consisted of blackboards and good old-fashioned pens and paper. I do chuckle when I think back to the teachers who had serious chalk dust marks on various parts of their clothing. I feel sorry for kids now; they never get the chance to laugh at "chalky teachers" anymore!

As a child, I was obsessed with technology and gadgets. Being born into a retailing family, I was used to working form the age of 15 and earning my own money so that I could buy the gadgets that I wanted. I used to save up my weekly wages from the newsagent where I worked, and buy the gadgets I wanted when I had saved the money.

I remember my first gadget was a ZX81 which was a small 'computer' with 1kB ram – those of you who are non-technical, this means that it had the memory and capabilities that are 500 times less than the phone that you have in your hand or on your desk now. The only use of the ZX81 was to plug into a black and white TV and play a very basic game.

The next gadget I bought was a Psion Series 3, which was portable computer; I suppose it is like a Netbook today. But again, the screen was black and white, and the functionality was limited.

I then moved on to many more gadgets as they were invented and released to the public. One important lesson I learnt was never to buy the first batch. The same applies today; the first batch of a new gadget is normally still full of bugs and issues – always wait a few weeks and buy the gadget after all the early bugs are fixed.

This love of gadgets moved on to mobile phones and pagers. In 1993, I was the proud owner of a 'Rabbit' phone – the most useless mobile phone invention. It worked as a cordless phone at home and when you went outside, you could make calls if you stood under an upside down 'R'; these were wireless connectors that made calls. You could never receive calls and the Rabbit died as quickly as it came along.

In 1994, Orange started a UK phone network and this is when I purchased my first mobile phone, the Motorola MR1. It could make and receive calls, but no texting back then.

As the technology grew in terms of devices, so did the connectivity and connections that we use to connect to the Internet. When I was at university, I was lucky enough to have the luxury of the Internet in my bedroom via ADSL. This meant that we had quick access to the Internet via a stable connection. Before this, we used dial-up which we all remember made a "whirring" sound as it connected and was painfully slow.

With all these new gadgets and new speeds to connect to the Internet, you would have expected me to have been the first adopter of Social Media. This was not the case as I did not want to be on any Social Media at the beginning. I am sure most of you have had, or still have, the same feelings.

With regard to Social Media, and more importantly with Facebook, I did not start using Facebook at the beginning when it was launched. I really did not want to be on Facebook or any Social Media network as I did not see the point.

This all changed when I went to live in the Czech Republic.  When you move away from your friends and family, you have to use electronic means to keep in contact.  I was emailing and making Skype calls and video calls, but I realised that I was telling my friends the same story on the phone, on video chat, on email.

I thought, "This is crazy," because I was not having a full conversation, I was just updating them on the general things that I had been doing. So I decided to look at Social Media and I joined Facebook, with no idea what it really was, but I had heard lots about it.  I was still not sure if I really want to share my life via an Internet page at this stage.

As soon as I took the step to go on to Facebook and set up my profile, I never looked back.  I made sure it was completely private, where only my friends could see me, only people that I wanted to be added as friends were added, and I shared lots things; I shared photos, updates, "check in"s etc.

When you are living abroad, you go to places that your friends have never been, you go to new places and you experience things that your friends have never experienced. But you have the innate desire to share all these new experiences with the people that you love. So, I started sharing my life on Facebook.

Once I started using Facebook consistently for my personal life, this made me think, "Well what is this bigger picture about? What is Social Media about?"

As a retailer, I was working in physical retail at the time, so it really opened my mind to think, "Well, this opens my life, I am communicating with people thousands of miles away daily, throughout the day."

I then looked at my business, where you physically have to come into the shop, walk in, exchange the money, take the products and go home. Whereas with this Amazon world, this whole e-commerce, e-tail and E-Revolution that is happening, you do not need to physically connect with your customers. This led me to start to learn how Social Media and e-commerce could change the way my businesses ran.

At this time, I was using Social Media personally, and I had to look at how does this Social Media work for a business and, more importantly, when I looked at writing my first book (*The Retail Handbook*), it was very much about the start of understanding Social Media for business.

Social Media was becoming a big part of my business life and in *The Retail Handbook*, I actually used Twitter hashtags for the important quotes and information. The idea was to enable people to share the quotes from the book and then interact on Twitter and start a conversation.

At the time I wrote the book, there was no precedent for using Social Media; I just tested the idea and then quickly saw that as a business and as a thought leader, Social Media was the way to go.

Since then, I have grown my personal and business presence on all the Social Media networks, and I now train people on Social Media and help people through the process of how to be seen as an expert, either as a business, as an author, or as a speaker.

## What surprised me when I started using Social Media

The most surprising change once I started using Facebook and the other Social Media channels, for me personally, was just the ease of sharing your life. You can post photos and updates on where you are and what you are doing, for your friends and family; this is a great way to keep in touch.

The sharing of your life also allows people to understand you more. As an author, this is important for you to acknowledge. When people are buying your book, they want to connect with and understand the author. The power of Social Media allows you to share your life with your community.

When I say "sharing", I mean opening yourself up privately. I keep all my Social Media networks private; I choose who I am friends with and who sees me, so this is not public. I am just opening that up within my circle of friends and family.

You can also open up your networks further, and with Facebook pages and other networks, Twitter especially, you can connect with people around the world. People that you just never would know physically, who can message you and say, "Hi, I read your book and I think it was great!"

So, the opening up of yourself and taking that step onto Social Media, will open up a new world of connections and experiences that you would just never ever get in a physical world.

It is impossible to have this amount of connections and exposure to new things and new ideas without Social Media. Social Media is truly a world and life-changing invention that every person and every business should utilise.

# Chapter 2: Why should you use Social Media?

## Why you must adopt Social Media

We have now passed a point where Social Media is an optional extra in your life or your business life – it is here and it offers amazing opportunities for you and your business.

Social Media is not a fad – it is not going to go away. The companies that are leading the Social Media world, the big worldwide companies, which are valued at billions of pounds, are growing and changing the world around you.

Social Media companies are big and powerful – they are worth hundreds of billions of pounds. A recent example of how big Social Media is, in terms of business deals, is when Facebook bought a messaging system for $16 billion. Now, $16 billion was what Ukraine needed to bail itself out of the problems. So Facebook in theory could have bought a country, which is a powerful place to be for any company.

Social Media and the companies that are leading this have so much money, so much influence, they are bigger and more powerful than countries. As far as I am concerned, if you are a person and more importantly a business, you need to join this; you need to get on to Social Media.

Even if you only use one of the Social Media sites, one blog or one Facebook page, you don't need to be on everything, but you need to get on to this now because in 10 years' time, Social Media will be a lot bigger and a lot more connected.

Companies and businesses that have adopted the world of Social Media are seeing big benefits in terms of business. Before Social Media, you would have been unlikely to connect with people within another town in your country and you are certain to be unable to connect with people in most countries around the world.

***Your world, personal and business,***
***will change when you start to use Social Media.***

You will become:

- More knowledgeable

- More connected

- Better known

- Better understood

- Known in places you have never been to

- Admired by your community

- An agent of change for people in your community

- A place where people come to for advice

- A place where you can support people across the world

- An expert in your passion/expertise for your community

## Grow your experiences and your world without the need to travel

If you are a person who wants to be a thought leader, and you have a message that you are passionate about, then Social Media is, as far as I am concerned, the only way to do that.

I often talk about my passions and expertise on E-Revolution, e-commerce, e-tailing and Social Media, and I find people talking to me and wanting me to connect with them across the world. I have had connections in Saudi Arabia, for example, where I have advised a number of large retail people, and in Croatia where I have spoken to their retailers who wanted to know about what we know in the UK and how we do things here.

As a thought leader, you become subsumed into this world of Social Media because you are learning more and more, each and every time you log on. There is so much information out there, and there are so many new, and interesting, ideas.

Your brain is continually thinking, "Ah, what about that? That is brilliant, I need to tell my people about that; I need to share this with my community."

Social Media really does open up a new world and a new way of thinking and understanding that you, as a thought leader, can really get your message out there to the world and share it.

We have always lived in a world where travel is said to broaden the mind. When people travel, their minds are broadened, and they, as people, are more aware of the world and their knowledge is far richer.

The amazing fact for us all to recognise, is that you have got all these potential experiences available to you now – by using Social Media. You do not need to get on a plane, you do not to get on a boat or a train. You do not need to travel to experience other cultures and other people that you can connect with and learn from.

You are a thought leader or a business leader, and you can connect with new people who are interested in your passion and your life.

People around the world will talk to you, because you have got something in common, so you can share a common language. The exciting and enriching part of this, is the fact that their culture is so different to yours. The value of this makes your community, in your world, so much more valuable and so much intriguing and interesting for your community.

Social Media is great for bringing information together; you bring your experiences and that information together for your community. You are adding value to them, you are adding value to your community, be that local or worldwide.

Social Media helps you grow as a person, as a business leader and retailer. All the time you are adding value to your community, you are improving their life and improving your own life through the Social Media.

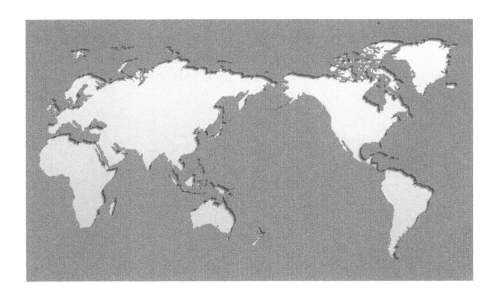

## It's not an "age thing"

Social Media is no longer age related and it has now become a tool for absolutely everybody, irrespective of age and experience.

There is a major preconception and misunderstanding with Social Media, which is that it is a "young person's thing". It may well have started in a university in terms of Facebook, the biggest Social Media network, but it did not stay in university.

This has helped fuel the idea, "If I am not young, I do not need to be on Social Media. It is not for me, it is for these younger people that are coming through," and this is absolutely not correct.

Social Media is for everyone. Yes, it is with younger people where it started, but the younger people have driven Social Media's growth, and those younger people have become working age. They have then started working and driving businesses, and they have set up businesses which allow us all to go global.

If you look at some of the statistics, especially for Facebook, the biggest growing part of the user base is the older generation, the 55+ age group, because what they are experiencing is that their kids who are in their thirties and forties are on Social Media, with maybe 50 per cent using Social Media, but their kids, or the grandkids, are absolutely 100% on Social Media.

If the grandparents are living in a different part of the country, or in a different country altogether, if they want to connect, or want to be part of the younger generation's life, which they do, they join Facebook and then they are getting all the benefits because they are realising that their friend who moved to Canada is also on Facebook and after 50 years they can chat, video chat, share messages and share photos.

So, the preconception that this is a young person's technology is absolutely false. It is for everybody and it adds value to every single person's life and, more importantly for businesses, it adds so much more to a business offering.

## Social Media brings together like minds

Social Media makes it possible to bring together like-minded people; people who have similar interests, beliefs, values, wants, needs and desires can all communicate together using Social Media, wherever they are in the world.

One of the biggest benefits of Social Media is that it brings together people who have an interest, who have a shared interest, or have shared likes in a way that we have never experienced before.

For example, imagine that your lifelong hobby is looking at, driving and researching vintage cars. We all know that there are lots of people in the world who love old vintage cars, and you can imagine the photographs and the videos of these vintage cars would be so exciting to these people.

In the world before Social Media, you would have joined a local vintage car club, but maybe you live in a part of the country, or a part of the world, where there are only two other people and there is only one vintage car. This would mean that your world and your hobby is vintage cars, but you can see one car and talk to one other person.  That would not give you the satisfaction you are looking for in a hobby.

Now, thanks to the world of Social Media, you could join groups and communities online with Social Media.  You can join groups where people who love vintage cars around the world are happy to chat to you and share stories and pictures. You could see vintage cars in Brazil, in Australia, in Peru, anywhere, and the power of this knowledge, and the enrichment of your life from this is immeasurable.

You cannot measure the difference to people's quality of life before Social Media and now in the world with Social Media. I have to reiterate that this will only grow as more people get online, more people share photos, more people share videos, more communities are formed, better technology is invented and faster connections are developed.

Take this experience into your world as a business owner, and you can start to see that by applying a few basic strategies and techniques, from this book, you can grow your own community of customers across the world. All of these people choose to hear your story and want to be involved in your community.

## Social Media has grown thanks to the developments in technology

Running in parallel with the growth of Social Media has been the incredible advance in mobile devices and network speeds; these two technological advancements have created the biggest uptake in Social Media since it began.

There has been an incredible advancement in technology, especially over the last three or four years. We used to be connected with a wire, and it used to make a strange noise when you had a dial-up connection and everything was slow. To get a picture downloaded was very painful... I remember it as a kid – it felt like years to download one photo.

We now have progressed through dial-up and fixed connections to 4G and Wi-Fi technology and superfast broadband. All these technologies are allowing us to get data faster, to interact quicker, to share videos and to get media on demand.

More importantly, the advancement in networks has allowed our world to become mobile. We are now seeing most people starting to have smartphones. Smartphones where we can chat, share photos, share your location and share videos at the touch of a button or the swipe of a screen.

The pace of change, and the E-Revolution, has brought about technology which has allowed us to be on the move connecting with people, sharing media, and Social Media is a conduit that makes that happen and enriches our mobile life – we no longer need to be static, sat in front of a device connected to a cable anymore.

## Social Media gives you choices

Social Media give you choices in life and in your business. The E-Revolution and the developments in Social Media has handed the power to make an informed decision to the users of Social Media and away from the corporations and governments.

Whatever you are doing in your life, you can research on the Internet and then use Social Media to interact and ask questions about the required knowledge you are looking for.

Let us take a holiday as an example. We all know that your holiday time is precious and you want to have the best time possible when you are on holiday.  When you are looking at places to visit, you need to research them and find out what they are like and what you can do there.

In the days before Social Media, we would have gone to a travel agent and chatted to them about what we were looking for.  They will have shown you a few brochures and you will have made a decision based on what they told you, and what the brochure told you.  Let us imagine that the travel agent is not a very honourable agency and they have a hotel in the place that you want to go to, which is not what you want, but they earn lots of commission from the hotel. Do you think the travel agent would tell you this fact, or do you think they would just tell you it is the perfect choice and book you in?  We like to think they would be honest, but let us be realistic – they are being paid to sell you a product.

Today, we buy our holidays totally differently. We use the Internet to search and, more likely, we go on Social Media and chat with our friends and community about where they go and what places are good. How many times do you see on Facebook, "Can anybody recommend a good hotel in xxxx?" or "I am thinking of visiting xxxx. Does anybody know any good places to visit?"

With Social Media, it is now possible to bypass the travel agent and book your own holiday exactly as you want it, with knowledge gained from your friends and your community – people who you trust.

And for that extra comfort factor, we now have Social Media platforms that allow you to rate your hotel, restaurant etc. This is a very powerful switch to giving the user of Social Media the power of choice and to make an informed decision.

In business, you can use the same principles to allow your customers to become better informed. Using Social Media will allow you to spread your message to customers who will start to trust and like you.

> ***Building a community, which allows people
> to be informed and make their own decision
> is powerful and what all businesses should aim for.***

# Chapter 3: The E-Revolution and Social Media for you as a business

## The E-Revolution

I would like to introduce the 'E-Revolution' and help you understand how the new world we live in, and do business in, has been made possible due to major changes in technology and e-commerce.

E-commerce businesses have used the Internet and Social Media to change our lives forever, and make our world a much more connected and technology-led environment. The speed of the growth with the Internet, the technologies and Social Media, which make up the E-Revolution, has allowed transactions to happen online. Once transactions started happening online, the business world we knew changed. Online transactions and trading has opened up a new world to all businesses.

We are now in a time when all businesses must start to utilise the world we now live in where e-transactions are common place and growing. There are different methods of the e-transactions happening – as a business, you can now sell your products and services across the world; you can download digital media from around the world; and you can research information all around the world.

Not only have e-transactions changed the world, connected and mobile devices have revolutionised the way we live our lives, both personal and business. We now have access to many different connected devices; they could be a desktop PC, mobile phone, tablet PC, laptop or any other connected device. For now, and the future, these mobile devices are where we can all order products and services.

Your customers can now download a podcast, they could download a PDF training guide, they could watch a video on how to do something, or they could order your physical products and get them delivered to their house or their office, or even the nearest train station.

*The E-Revolution is allowing every business
to transact mobile-wise and technically-wise
anywhere in the world at anytime.*

## The E-Revolution has changed the world of business

One of the biggest benefits for businesses, and people sharing messages, is that the old world and the 'old boys' networks' have disappeared.

If you look at the music industry, the film industry and at publishing books, the E-Revolution and the 'e-business' pioneers like Amazon have changed the way we interact and purchase our goods and services.

In the past, if you wanted to publish a book, you would have to go to a publishing house; you would have to go through their process – you would have to, in essence, impress them. This was the same if you wanted a record deal or to become a TV star.

The world has now changed and you can publish a book yourself online, easily, quickly and with you in control. For example, Amazon have the capability to publish a book straightaway online and if you want to produce physical books, there are a lot of new services available which allow you to publish a physical book across the world on your own.

The E-Revolution allows you to share and promote your products and services all over the world via the Internet and Social Media. The challenge now is that whilst it is a lot easier now to "share" your products and services online, business owners need to understand how to generate the demand for the products. Otherwise they are just going to sit there – nobody will know about your business or your products.

You need to know how to market your products and services, and how to sell these in the new world of the E-Revolution. It is the same with any part of your business; you need to find out where your customer "is" and what Social Media channels they use as part of their customer journey.

You could, and I am sure you have, the most amazing products and services, but if you do not sell these and market these in the correct channels, nobody will ever find your products in the massive ocean of competition.

*We are in a new world,*
*and a new way of selling products and marketing products*
*using the online Social Media model.*

## Bring your business to life using Social Media

The E-Revolution gives you a new way of thinking and operating your business. You have lots of new technology, devices and Social Media – all of which combine to give you, as a business owner, the tools to market your business and services to a worldwide audience.

You need to add life to your products and services and bring your message into the Social Media world – bring your business "alive". You need to add videos, you need to add photos, you need to share the understanding of your products and services using Social Media.

If you run a services business (such as a consultancy, training company or advisory business), you can use Social Media to share the content behind your business. Your business is founded on unique methods and systems; sharing the concept of these will help your customers to understand what you do and why you do it. You can do this by giving away knowledge gifts.

Using Social Media to give these knowledge gifts allows people who are interested from around the world to start to connect with you, with a little video or a free download, or a podcast or a model. Your target customer will then start to come into your world and join your community.

Bringing your customers into your community means that you can then interact with them, and share with them on a more personal basis, even though they could be thousands of miles away. This is powerful and helps you grow your business extensively and globally.

## Changes in technology and fear

In life, most people fear change and there is a big fear of the E-Revolution, Social Media, the Internet, mobile devices etc, across the world. I believe the fear is driven because of the speed of the changes in technology, systems and devices. It is only a small number of years, measurable on two hands, that Social Media has been around, and we have progressed from using a computer to chat, to using a laptop, to now walking around with different devices. We are even going to have watches and glasses to communicate and use Social Media. This speed of change takes people into fear mode.

You must understand that Social Media is not a fad; Social Media is here to stay. It is an intrinsic part of the world. Whoever thinks it is going to go away will not succeed long term. Social Media will stay, and it will only grow because more people want to be connected.

*We have an innate desire to be part of communities*
*and to interact –*
*Social Media is that conduit.*

Social Media is going to continue to happen. It is a case of accepting that social Media is here and then using it, because once you get on to it, the things that you can do and the things that you can see and find out are amazing.

You can see and experience things around the world that you would never see as a normal person flying around the world. By trying Social Media, just going online, just dipping your feet into the online world, into Social Media, trying a couple of sites, setting up a profile.

You will quickly start to see that there is so much out there, and that will take you into the new Social Media world. I promise you will enjoy it and it will enrich your personal life, as well as your business life.

## The world of "search"... Just Google it

Another area that runs in parallel with Social Media is what the search engines now make possible. We have all started to use the Internet and we all use the search engines, mainly Google. Whenever we need to know something, the first thing we do is look it up online, and that is the new start of our search for knowledge and information.

The E-Revolution and Social Media have meant that you almost have to have a presence online to 'exist'. I would argue that in fact you MUST have a presence online and this is because we all hear the phrase "just Google it".

If anybody wants to gain any knowledge, they will now automatically open Google and search for their interest and the information they need. This could be looking for a restaurant, looking for a new pair of trousers or searching for holiday destinations. Whatever we want to know, we can "Google" it.

If you as a person, and you more importantly as a business, are not online, you do not have a website, a blog, a Facebook profile, or a LinkedIn profile, then people cannot find you.

*Having a presence on the Internet is a must for every business, and Social Media profiles are the cheapest and simplest way to establish an online presence.*

The world is changing and whenever we do anything, because we all have smartphones, we arrive somewhere and we search. We find out what there is in the area.

If we need to learn anything, for example what is it like to live in a country or town, what is the best restaurant, how do I use this technology, or how do I write a book... we would instantly search for it.

So as a business, you need to be online and have a presence.  If you are not online, you will not be found and you do not exist for people looking for your products and services.

## Social Media is real two-way communication

I like to describe Social Media as "the physical world online". With Social Media, you can chat and interact with your friends, just like you would when you meet them in the local coffee shop. Social Media allows, and encourages, conversation to happen between people.

When you grow your Social Media networks and develop your own communities, you will see the power of having a network of people in your community who want to interact with you and want to learn from you.

The fact that they can talk to you, and you can talk to them, shows that we are in a new world where online Social Media communities can learn and interact just like a physical community.

For the first time, we have a global way to have two-way communications using all the media and devices you want. You can share words, text, images and videos across your community and the globe. You can share, like, comment and update your content for your communities across the world.

The E-Revolution has given birth to a new world of real two-way communication across borders and continents.

# Chapter 4: Content and keywords are key

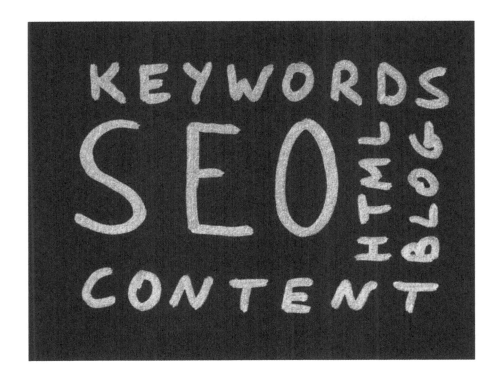

## Content is key, and keywords are your key to success

Welcome to the chapter where I cover content and keywords. These are very important for Social Media. There is a process to create great content and keywords, which I cover later in the chapter.

Content is the information that you share with your customers via Social Media networks and other media. This includes all you say, write, film, produce and the images that you use in your marketing and in your business.

One of the most important concepts and understandings that you need to have as a business, is that:

### *Content is key*

When you are using Social Media, having good quality, relevant content is an absolute must. You can only build a large and engaged community with lots of relevant and quality content.

> All content needs to be:
>
> - Relevant – Ensure your content is relevant to your audience. Ensure the topic is what they are wanting to hear about and that you share this in the right communities.
> - Timely – Some content is very timely i.e blogs on events that are happening, and need to be shared at a point in time where it will have the most impact.
> - Good Quality – Make sure every piece of content you share with your community is of good quality, and reflects you and your business well.
> - Engaging – You are trying to build a community, and to do that you need to be engaging. Your content needs to engage with your community, and allow them to interact and engage with you.

## How to make great content for your customers

Make your content perfect for your customers and the search engines:

- **Know your brand (your style of writing)**
  You must ensure that you always write in the style of your brand. Over time, your community get to know your brand style – they trust and become comfortable with it. This should be reflected in everything you do, from the tone of your emails, to the wording in your tweets, to the colours in your pictures.

- **Know your customer**
  Knowing your customer is key. If you do not know them well enough, you will not be able to interact with them in a way that fits their wants, needs and desires.

- **Ensure keywords are included**
  Understanding your keywords is critical to generating content – you must research them well and use them in every tweet, blog and Facebook update.

## Tips for creating and gathering content

Gathering content for your business takes time, and you also need to gather ongoing content for your communities and your online world. Here are some tips for making and gathering compelling content that will speak to your readers:

- **Treat your readers like VIPs**
  - People who subscribe to your Social Media networks have given you an indication that they are interested and want to engage with you. Honour this by letting them be the first to know about new products, special offers or sales. Give them access to special benefits as subscribers.

- **Keep it useful**
  - Think about the messages and posts that you read and you do not read - you do not read a post that does not benefit or interest you in some way. Make sure the title and content of your content are giving your followers something they did not have before.

- **Show some personality**
  - Nobody wants to read dry, boring updates – inject some personality. Your voice, tone and sense of humour are all important reasons why your customers followed you in the first place.

- **Keep it short**
  - We are all bombarded with messages every day. Keep your updates short, easy to digest, and to the point.

- **Get inspired**
  - Keep a note of things that interest you and would therefore interest your customers. Use a notepad, or to be more digital, use an app - great for saving, organising and accessing content to use in your updates at a later time.

## Keywords

....and with content, you must use and understand keywords.

### *Keywords:*
### *are the words that your customers use*
### *to find you online and on Social Media networks*

When you use a search engine, when you look at any sort of search function on any website on the Internet, you need to have a set of keywords that describe your business. These are common to your business across the board and are the descriptive words used to describe you and your business.

As a retailer, I see everything from a retail perspective, and being part of a retail family, I have always been aware of keywords. In the past, we used to have 'keywords' clearly showing – if you can imagine a High Street, where we have signs outside the shops, that is in essence a keyword. As you walk down the street, you see a greengrocer, butcher, baker and candlestick maker in the good old days. When you saw these signs, you immediately knew what they sold and what was inside the shop.

On the previous page is a photo of my great-grandfather's shop in the 1920s. As you can see, on the left his 'keyword' was "Bacon Specialist", as he ran a provisions shop and he was the south-east importer of Danish bacon – his keyword and market niche.  ou can also see that there was a butcher and, on the right, a printers.

In the same way, your Social Media world needs to have keywords, and those keywords that you used to see on a High Street need to be online and on your Social Media profiles.

When you are writing any content, if you are writing just a tweet, which is 140 characters, or if you are writing a Facebook update, or a blog, then having content that is relevant and good quality, but with keywords included, is an absolute must.

Using keywords in all your content means that people can find your message and understand that you are talking about a certain topic, which they can find using the search functions. You must ensure that they can find your video because it has the keywords, they find your blog because it has the keywords, they find your Facebook page because it has the keywords.

This is why keywords are so important and why they really do fundamentally underpin everything that you as a person, and as a business, do online and on Social Media.

## How to find your keywords

How to find your keywords is probably the question that I get asked the most often, and there is no one single answer. There are a few places where you can find them.

The first place I always start with is to ask your customers. Your customers are the people who are buying your product or service, and they will have a set of words that they use when they are looking for your product or service.

You must find out what words your customers use when they are looking for you. What do they actually physically type into Google? From understanding this information, you will gain a set of words that your customers use to find you.

From this knowledge, you can then really funnel down to the exact keywords that you want to be known for and you are setting your business up for. Again, let's go back to think about a High Street and shops. People know what a greengrocer is and they will look down the street to find this shop. So your keywords would say: 'fruit,' 'vegetables,' 'fresh,' 'available,' etc.

The key task is to really get down to the words that people use to describe your business, and just expanding those slightly to really refine the exact messages that you are trying to give, and the exact products and services that you are actually trying to sell.

The simple keyword model:

1. Ask your customers/community what words they use to find you and discuss you.

2. Research the market – look at your competitors and other people that are in your field.

3. Use the Google Keyword Tool (see later in this chapter).

4. Test the keywords on your market (see the strategy chapter for more details).

5. Use the keywords in all your content.

6. Adapt your keywords with time, and with new products and services.

## Is there a restriction on the number of keywords that you can use?

In terms of the number of keywords that you should use, there is no restriction. You can have a million keywords if you want, but it would not work at all if you had that many; this would defeat the object of defining keywords to be 'key'.

The ideal number of keywords is probably three to four because people type into Google two to five words and your goal is to be found with those keywords.

For example, if you run an e-commerce business and you are writing about e-commerce and e-commerce training, there are probably three words that you would want to be known for and talk about: e-commerce, training, online.

Having a small number of keywords is important, so that everything that you do, everything that you write online, should have those keywords in, and too many keywords will make writing good content difficult.

It is also important to bear in mind that from a very technical website point of view, on your website and on your blog, you need to have these words. This is called SEO (search engine optimisation) and best practice suggests that keywords should be in the title and in other parts of the website.

This is because Google (and other search engines) will look at these words and see if the website, the blogs and the Social Media content are all in line. This is important, as searching on Google will show your details and you want to be found for your keywords in this search.

You want to be found all over the web searches so that the search engines will say, "This person is always talking about e-commerce – I can see it because it is in the title of his website, it is in every blog that he talks about and it is in his tweets. Therefore, this person must be an expert and must know about e-commerce."

The reality is, if you do not include keywords in all your online and Social Media channels, no matter how beautiful your site, no matter how pretty the colours and lovely graphics, it will be totally invisible to people who are looking for it.

Not having good keywords will make you invisible. You will not be found if you do not have good keywords and use them consistently; people will not find you. You will not be on the top one or two pages of Google search, which is where we normally all start our search.

Your role and your goal should be for your keywords to be the top page or the top two pages of Google, or YouTube, or other search engines.

## Tools to help you find your keywords

In terms of a technical process, once you believe you know what your keywords are, once you have spoken to your customers and carried out your research, you can use the keyword tool that is on Google.

Anybody can sign up to a Google account; it is very simple to open a Google account, then you can just search for the keyword tool and it will tell you how to do it.  In this tool, part of the programme that Google runs, it tells you how many people search for your chosen keywords.

You can, for example, if you are a physical business and you are selling shirts, type in shirts and it will tell you that quite a few million people each day search for shirts.  So you do not want to compete with millions of other websites.  You want to compete with a smaller number of competitors and that would be more focused keywords. You could try a couple of keywords together, maybe luxury or white shirts. The keyword tools will tell you the number of people who search for these keywords.

Finding your perfect keywords is a process of elimination, of finding your best keyword combination. It is a combination of what your customer searches for, of what you know about your own business and then using these keyword tools to see what the people on the Internet do, what they search for; the Google Keyword Tool is probably the best place for that.

### Hashtags #

In the last part of this section, I would like to introduce you to the world of hashtags (#). These are keywords that people use on Twitter and Facebook to search and use as a 'theme'.

Many people will use # on Twitter during a conversation – you may have heard the phrase 'trending on Twitter'. This means that many people are talking about that # (or keyword). For example, during a public event, people will be chatting about it i.e. #LondonOlympics.

Alternatively, when people have had a bad customer experience they will tweet the company – "I bought some shoes from xxx shop and they were rubbish #fail"

Hashtags are a very open and very clear use of keywords and mainly used on Twitter and Facebook.

# Chapter 5: The basic anatomy of a Social Media network

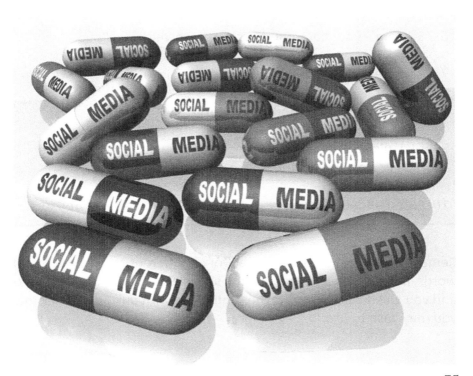

## All Social Media networks follow a similar format

Social Media networks have all developed significantly over the last few years and they are all different in a number of ways. They do, however, share a very similar anatomy irrespective of their own words and their own purpose.

There is a basic anatomy of Social Media networks that I will discuss with you over the next few pages.

1. Profile page

2. Business/Book/Product/Company pages

3. Friends and Connections

4. Timelines/Activity page

5. Groups

6. Sharing – your community getting involved

7. Commenting - your community getting involved

8. Chatting – a more one-to-one world

9. Likes/Follows/Friends – people and things that you like – movies, food, places, people etc

10. Posts/Updates/Check ins – your individual posts and updates

Remember, every Social Media network is different and uses different words, but the principles remain the same. Start with these networks and you will quickly discover the similarities with any other ones that you may wish to use.

New Social Media networks will always be starting up over the next few years, and I will keep these up to date in later editions and in my online communities.  For now, we will concentrate on the main eight networks.

## Profile page

This is the page that has all the facts about you, your images, your text and your videos etc. This is the first page that people will read when they search for you on the Social Media networks.

This page is the start of every Social Media network. At the beginning, you need to set up a profile. A profile is basically the 'About you' page where you share the details about yourself.

At this stage, you can share as much or as little as you want, but there are some basics needed for you to be able to communicate with and be a part of that social network.

All networks require you to set up a profile as a person in the beginning; you can then set up a profile as a busines.

---

The basics you would want to share on your profile page as a business are:

1.  Name
2.  Location
3.  Profile picture (of yourself, not your brand)
4.  Cover photo (a larger photo which fits the width of a monitor screen, used to give a visual understanding of yourself)
5.  Job title/Business purpose
6.  Contact details
7.  Likes, activities and interests

---

The likes, activities and interests section of any Social Media network is important to complete. This section allows people to search for you on that Social Media network via these keywords. Although these are not strictly keywords, as we have discussed earlier, these words and phrases will help people understand you and understand the community you are trying to build.

The rest of the profile is more bespoke to the Social Media network and can include many different pieces of information.

Here are two examples of profiles from Facebook and LinkedIn.

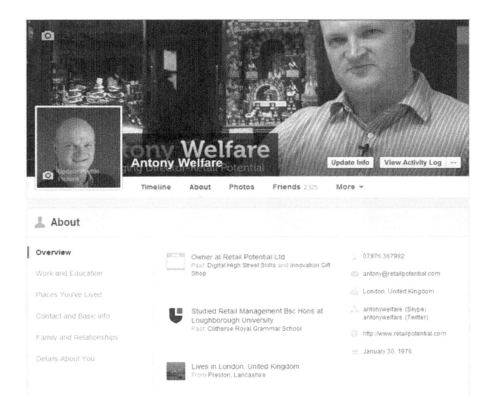

**Linked**  ®

## Antony Welfare
Ecommerce Professional
London, United Kingdom | Retail

| | |
|---|---|
| Current | **Ecommerce Strategy Consultant** at **SmartWeaveStore.com** |
| | **Managing Director** at **Innovation Gift Shop** |
| Past | Digital National Manager at Digital High Street UK |
| | Managing Director/Finance Director at TV Discount Store Ltd |
| | Ecommerce and Finance Director at Bolongaro Trevor |
| | see all ˅ |
| Education | Loughborough University |
| Recommendations | **13** people have recommended Antony |
| Connections | **500+** connections |
| Websites | Company Website |
| | Blog |

Antony Welfare's Summary

Antony Welfare is a Retail, Ecommerce and Social Media professional with over 20 years industry experience with international multi-channel retailers such as Marks & Spencer, Sainsburys, Dixons Retail and Homebase.

Antony has launched 3 brand new Ecommerce businesses and relaunched two fashion brand Ecommerce businesses, as well as working on developing the Dixons Ecommerce businesses from the beginning.

As you can see, there is some similar key information and then much more detail on certain parts of you.

It is important to stress that as a business owner, you must share as much information as possible. Once you start to share to your Social Media community, new people will be joining your network and they need to know as much about you as possible. I tend to share as much information as I can about me; that way, I know anybody new looking at my profiles will gain a good understanding of me and this will help them understand my community.

Privacy is a key concern on any Social Media network and I would always say to share the information and images you are comfortable to share, and only 'friend' and 'connect' with people who you know and want to be part of your community.

## Business/Book/Product/Company pages

Once you have set up your own personal profile, you then need to set up a business page.

Different Social Media networks name these differently:

| | | |
|---|---|---|
| **Facebook** | - | Page |
| **Twitter** | - | They do not offer this ability (set up a second profile) |
| **Linkedin** | - | Company Page |
| **Youtube** | - | Channel |
| **Pinterest** | - | They do not offer this ability (set up a second profile) |
| **Instagram** | - | They do not offer this ability (set up a second profile) |
| **Google+** | - | Page |

For Facebook, Linkedin, Youtube and Google+, you can set up a business page for your business. This is important to do, because this will allow you to focus your community on your products and build a clear community around that.

## Friends and Connections

Your friends and your connections are the people you choose to be connected to on the Social Media network and people who choose to be friends and connections with you. These are your community and the reason you are using Social Media.

As a person profile, you have to accept a friend request or send a friend request. This is set up to make sure that you only connect with people you know, or you have something in common with.

As a business page, people will 'like' or 'follow' you. This means they choose to read your business timeline and they choose to interact with you and your business. You do not have to be friends with these people, so you can keep your friends and connections to people you really know.

This is the main reason why setting up a business page is an important part of the Social Media networks. Pages carry limited personal information and do not allow personal connections. This means you can happily post information to your page that is solely for your business and you do not need to be their friend.

## Timelines/Activity page

With a profile or a page, you have a timeline or activity page. This is where you tell your community what you are doing, share content and engage in conversations. This is the key page on any Social Media network.

On this page, you will share your content and share your ideas. There are many different ways to share, and different media to share. I will discuss Facebook as this is the biggest and most comprehensive Social Media network. The principles are easily applied to the other Social Media networks.

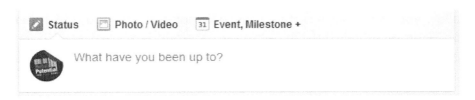

Here is a very standard view on most Social Media networks. This is where you share your content with your community.

The first way to share content is via the 'status' update; this can cover anything you want and will show on your timeline. In this, you can add links to websites as well as comments.

The usual method to use this status is to share a few lines about a subject that you are discussing. In the strategy section, I discuss how to write and split the content down for each Social Media network.

In the status update, you can also share videos and photos, as well as add events and milestones. All of these updates will be shared with your community of people who like or follow the page.

Having a strategy for content sharing is important; if you just share random and unfocused content, you will lose your community. They follow you for a reason and your content must be written and shared for your community.

## Groups

Setting up groups on the Social Media networks is very important for building a community. Once you have built your profile and built your business profile or page, you then need to allow your community to interact with you.

Pages allows this to happen as your community can comment, share, like and message you, but you may want to go the next step and set up groups. These work especially well in LinkedIn, where you can join groups and really chat with like-minded people on a topic.

Groups can be set up on Facebook, LinkedIn and Google+, and they all allow you to discuss a certain topic (the point of the group) in either an open or private forum. Setting up a group is a great way to get people involved and discussing your products and services.

The difference between a page and a group is that a group allows a deeper interaction via significantly more sharing of ideas, documents, opinions, polls etc. Groups are a great way to manage an active community and get lots of engagement. A page is more 'static' and used for an easier and simpler level of engagement.

## Comments

Your aim on Social Media is to build an engaged community, and to do this, you would like to gain comments from your community relevant to the content that you share and post.

The art of getting your community involved via comments is a difficult journey, but one that this book will help you to achieve. The main point to remember is to make sure what you post allows your community to interact and comment on it. Ask your community questions or share thoughts that make your community think about it and want to comment.

Here is how you comment on content on a few of the main Social Media networks:

### Facebook: Comment

### Twitter: Reply

### LinkedIn: Comment

Like · Comment · Share · 30m ago

### Google+: Add a comment

+1   ➔   Add a comment...

## Likes

The introduction of the 'Like' button came from the Social Media networks and is an easy way for any user to say, "I like this piece of content". It is used as a measure of how interesting or engaging a piece of content is.

As a community builder, you want to build a community with lots of content that is shared, commented on and liked. Out of the three options, 'liked' is the most passive form of engagement.

You will find that your community will easily 'like' your content, but to gain more engagement by comments or shares, you need to refine and test your content.

Here is how you 'like' content on a few of the main Social Sedia networks:

### Facebook: Like

### Twitter: Favourite

Reply  Retweet  ★ Favorite  ••• More

### LinkedIn: Like

Like · Comment · Share · 30m ago

### Google+: +1

## Sharing content

This is the main part of Social Media for you as a business is sharing content. Sharing content is the key to growing your community and getting your community involved. We have discussed how to create good content in a previous chapter, and the importance of great and relevant content cannot be forgotten.

Sharing content on any Social Media website is easy. This is what they were set up to do. Once you have joined the network and set up your profiles and pages, your sharing of content is easy for your community.

Here is how you share content on a few of the main Social Media networks:

### Facebook: Share

### Twitter: Retweet

### LinkedIn: Share

### Google+: The arrow button

There are many ways to help make sharing content easier and these are covered in the next section where I discuss the main Social Media networks.

# Chapter 6: The Social Media channels for a business

## The Social Media Interaction Model

Before I take you into an in depth guide to the Social Media networks, I want to introduce the concept of the Social Interaction Model. This model will help take you from an unengaged community to an engaged community.

An engaged community is one which is likely to buy your products and services. Spending the time developing an engaged community will allow you to sell your products and services easily.

In this model, we are trying to take your community to the 'Interactors' area. This is because these are the networks where your community can interact with you and other members of your community.

Not all Social Media networks are good at interacting. Some are great to 'feed' your community with small pieces of content and send them to your interactor networks to really build a solid and engaged community.

There are many Social Media networks that I am introducing, but I categorise these networks into two types:

1. 'Feeder' Social Media networks
2. 'Interactor' Social Media networks

This concept is important to understand, as this will drive the behaviour and the way you manage the Social Media networks that you use.

1. The 'Feeder' networks

These networks are the networks that you use to 'feed' your communities which will interact with you in the 'Interactor' networks. A 'Feeder' network often uses limited characters, limited images and does not allow significant interaction.

2. The 'Interactor' networks

These networks are the heart of your communities. You 'live' in these networks with your communities and interact on a deep basis with them.

## The Social Media Interaction Model explained

There are two measures of the Social Media Interaction Model:

1. Depth of interaction – The ability to connect with your audience on a meaningful basis, with lots of content and information.

2. Strength of connection – The strength of the connection as measured by the ability to interact fully, and share information, opinions and data, and build a real community.

**What does all this mean?**

The way I view Social Media networks is based on the two axis of interaction and connection. The aim of Social Media for your business is to build and develop an engaged community.

To build the community, you need to 'feed' the community and expand your reach as far as possible – the 'Feeder' networks. Once you have 'fed' your social networks and gained followers on the 'Feeder' networks, you then need to take these people and engage with your community on the 'interactor' networks.

All Social Media networks are 'feeders' and there is a scale to which they become more and more engaged.

Your goal is to use the 'Feeder' networks to get your message out to a wide audience and use the 'Interactor' networks to build and interact with your community.

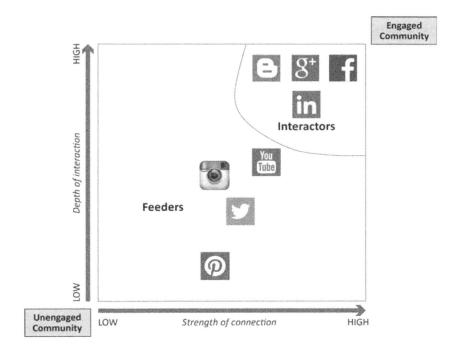

You need to build your main community in the 'Interactor' area. These Social Media networks are the networks where you have the best connection and best depth of interaction with your community.

Here are the eight main networks I recommend and the Social Media networks we will discuss in detail on the following pages.

| Social Media Channel | Logo | Website | Feeder or Interactor |
|---|---|---|---|
| Facebook | | www.facebook.com | Interactor |
| Blogs | | Various | Interactor |
| Twitter | | www.twitter.com | Feeder |
| YouTube | | www.youtube.com | Feeder |
| LinkedIn | | www.linkedin.com | Interactor |
| Pinterest | | www.pinterest.com | Feeder |
| Instagram | | www.instagram.com | Feeder |
| Google+ | | www.google+.com | Interactor |

## The different Social Media channels/platforms that are available now

In terms of Social Media platforms, there are a very large number of providers that you can use. However, for businesses, there are four or five that are key, and there are eight that I would recommend.

I would suggest to every business to try and have a presence on all of them. Not only does this allow you to gain a more diverse community, it helps with the SEO and helps the search engines to find you. The more profiles you have, the more places you will be found and the better this will make your SEO (search engine optimisation – this is basically making your business and your website more easily found in the search engines and on the Internet).

Within the following few pages, I will discuss the main eight Social Media networks that I recommend for businesses, and I will take you through what they are used for and how to use them to build your communities.

Having a number of networks allows you to cater for the different types of people in your community. Some of your customers may prefer to connect on Twitter, some may prefer LinkedIn groups. It is therefore important to understand which networks your customers use, because these are the networks that are the most important to your business.

Whichever your customers are using, whatever they connect with best, use those ones more than the ones that you prefer. Remember, this is not about you, this is about what your customers want and how they want to interact with you in the Social Media world.

## Blogs

The first Social Media network I always talk about is a blog, and a blog is a very simple platform. It's normally hosted on a programme like WordPress or Blogger (which Google own). A blog is not strictly known as a Social Media network, but it is the foundation of what you share on Social Media networks, and is the glue that binds together your Social Media networks and your community.

It is also important to understand that by blog, I mean the website where you host your longest and most interesting articles. This is also very likely to be your website, or be a big part of your website. A blog and a website will allow you to share knowledge gifts, allow interactions and sell products and services to your customers.

A blog is basically a place where you are sharing your messages in around about one page in length, maybe five to ten paragraphs.

It is the place where you write about your subject matter, all of it or just one part of it. For example, a blog could be a topical story, it could be how to do something, it could be showcasing your latest product, introducing the latest person in your team, discussing your latest service offering etc.

A blog is about writing to your customers and informing them about you and your business. Great blogs look at your opinions and ideas, and they bring to life your business.

When writing any blog, make sure that you use your keywords. Whatever your keywords are, which you have already discovered in previous chapters, make sure that they are represented somewhere in the blog.

Once you are happy with your blog, you can then publish and share the blog. Writing a blog is really where you start the Social Media journey and this is the easiest part in terms of what we are already used to. We are already used to writing quite long paragraphs about a topic, about a subject, and this is all a blog is.

Blogging is the start of sharing your content and is key to building a great community. There is a much more comprehensive look at the blogging at the next section.

| Social Media Channel | What it's used for | Examples of use |
|---|---|---|
| **Blogs** | • Blogs are used to share articles, information, research and opinions of your community.<br><br>• Share longer blogs about your area of knowledge, what's happening with your business, and your products and services.<br><br>• Share your opinions on world events, things that are happening in your world that will interest your community. | • Share your opinion on the latest news in your industry.<br><br>• Show your latest products and discuss the thinking behind the range.<br><br>• Introduce your latest offers and why they are relevant to the customers.<br><br>• Share a video of customers using your products and services.<br><br>• Update your customers on your latest additions to your business services.<br><br>• Upload a few photographs from your latest trip. |

## Facebook

The second Social Media network which I advise people to use is Facebook and particularly Facebook pages for business profiles. As an individual, you have a Facebook profile, but as a business, you can set up a page. By doing this, you can separate your personal life and your business life.

It is very much your choice whether you use the profile as your means of having a presence on Facebook, or whether you use a page. As a person (with a profile), you have to 'friend' people and they have to 'friend' you.  As a page, anybody can like and follow your page. I would recommend that as a business, you have a page, and as a person, you have a personal profile on Facebook.

The main idea with Facebook is to share messages, or images and videos. Write a few sentences, add a few images. or add a video of something of interest, and build up a set of updates, photos and videos.  You can also share links to other websites, blogs, videos etc. This is a great way to grow your community by sharing content that you like and commenting on that content.

Another great benefit with Facebook is that you can join communities and groups, as Facebook calls them. You can set up a group on your book using your keywords and start interacting with people. These groups can be private or they can be public.  You can have a conversation with your community in private, or you can have an open conversation where other people can join in.  The idea is really to build a community to get people liking, sharing and just joining in the discussions on the platform.

When you have a Facebook page, people have to 'like' the page. You should only post, on the page, information that you want to be free and what you want people to know and interact with. You cannot make your page private, so it is important to know that what you post on your page will be seen by the world.  Make sure you post good, intelligent content.

In summary, Facebook has three types of presence:

| Facebook Presence | Purpose | Privacy options | How to Connect? |
|---|---|---|---|
| **Profile** | This is where you as a person have your information and share your own life. | This can be very private and there are various levels of privacy and interaction. | You have to request connection as a friend.<br><br>You can follow a profile, which means you get limited updates from that person. |
| **Page** | This is where you set up a page for the world to see on your business, topic, subject, business etc. | This is open and people can interact on the page. | You can 'like' a page and then follow it. |
| **Group** | This is set up for a group of people to interact and share information. | Public or private. | You request to join a group. |

## Advantages of Facebook

- Largest and most crowded. Facebook is the most crowded and congested Social Media site on the Internet. With the recent update of over a billion subscribers, Facebook is only second to Google in terms of online traffic.

- You can quickly gain a large community. Facebook users continue to grow each day which makes building a community here reach a large number of users in a very short time.

- You can connect with everyone. The user base cuts across geography, education, experience, age, sex, religion or culture.

- Everybody is on Facebook. Business people, individuals, religious crusaders and fun makers are all on Facebook for various reasons. This makes Facebook a place where you can keep up with anyone, and the connections are easy.

- Once you click on a link, all your friends get informed. When you are doing any book promotion on Facebook, you have the advantage of reaching many people when one person likes the post. Once one person clicks 'like' to a link, all his/her friends are informed at once about the update.

- Great analytical features. Facebook includes a data analytics function that informs subscribers of everything that is happening on their page and the page of their friends.

- Varied and complex privacy controls. Users are able to use custom settings that determine how they want to be seen or found on the site.

- Easy to navigate. Facebook is easy to use because all the features about sharing information are just a click away.

- Facebook Mobile and apps. Facebook is continually developing its access points and develops many apps to help you communicate with other Facebook users more easily and when you are on the go.

**Disadvantages of Facebook**

- Only one main profile. You can only set up one profile page which means there is no separation of personal and professional side of your life.

- Varied and complex privacy controls. The privacy and sharing controls are great, but because of the large numbers of users, the security settings change often and privacy can be at risk if you do not keep up with the latest changes.

- Facebook Mobile and apps. Facebook is continually developing its access points and develops many apps to help you communicate via Facebook. This could become cumbersome and some apps do not work well.

| Social Media Channel | What it's used for | Examples of use |
|---|---|---|
| **Facebook** | • Facebook is the main Social Media network.<br><br>• Used daily by millions of people to keep in touch, share photos and interact.<br><br>• View Facebook as you would view talking to your friends face-to-face. | • Upload professional and business photographs.<br><br>• Share images of your new product ranges.<br><br>• Update your page with your latest new services.<br><br>• Show the latest promotions and offers.<br><br>• Promote an event to your community. |

## Twitter

The third Social Media network that I would like to introduce is Twitter. Twitter is a Social Media network where you write very short messages, 140 characters only, and these are called 'tweets'. This means your message has got to be very simple and to the point.

Twitter is a great way to 'grab attention' for people in your community. It will test your writing skills to make such a short, but impactful message. You can add images to the tweet, which is a great way to add more to a short message, and images are often more useful than words.

Twitter is very much used for the one-liners to hook people onto your website, to your blog and maybe to your Facebook page. You should look at Twitter as basically saying, "Look at this, this is happening," or "Did you know this? Some interesting facts, interesting links, interesting photos etc."

On Twitter, you have got a few milliseconds to grab somebody's attention and literally it should be the shortest sentence you can imagine, but still content rich and in line with your brand voice. You must make sure that as a business you try not to sell too much, try not to be, "Buy my latest service, buy my latest product". People do not like being sold to directly; they like to join your community, be a part of you, get to know you and then you can sell through different methods later.

I would not advise directly selling continually on Twitter, but you should do some selling of your business services. For example, out of my tweets, there are probably one in ten that are sales ones. The main purpose of Twitter is to use it for messages to gain interest in your community and to 'hook people' into wanting to know more.

One of the great benefits of Twitter is that you do not have to friend another person; you can follow anybody you want on Twitter. This is a big opportunity for you as a business owner. If you would like to communicate with a thought leader in another country, you can send a message to them directly or you can comment on their tweets.

Good Twitter etiquette suggests that if you want to connect with a person, follow them and understand their messages. When they post a tweet of interest, retweet it (i.e share it) and then send a response or reply to them.

On Twitter, you can follow people and they will follow you. Another tip for the good Twitter etiquette is to follow people who follow you. It seems it is polite to follow people back if they are interested in your message. I would do this with caution; make sure you follow people you want to, not just people who follow you.

The final point to make about Twitter is to help you understand the Twitter feed. This is the place where you see all the tweets from people who you follow. If you have a few people that you follow, it will be a slow-moving Twitter feed, but when you follow hundreds and thousands of people, you will see that your feed has thousands of messages on it. This is important to understand, because it means that you only have milliseconds to read a tweet from people you follow.

Think about this when you are tweeting; if your follower is following 2,000 other people, they are unlikely to see your tweet. This is where I advise that you share your tweets more than just the once. One share of a tweet will be unread by a large proportion of your followers.

I use an automated system to send out my basic tweets (covered at the end of this chapter). By doing this, I know my community will see my messages at some stage in the tweeting cycle.

**Advantages of Twitter**

- Easy to follow topics and issues. With Twitter, there is an easy use of hashtags (#) when a user intents to follow on a certain topic.

- Posts are brief. There is a limit to character usage that makes sure posts are only short. This way, it is easy to find the information you need.

**Disadvantages of Twitter**

• Brief posts. While this appears as an advantage in terms of scanning the message you want, many people do not like it. It is not possible to conclusively address an issue and have a conversation on Twitter.

• Missed posts information. If you have a huge following on Twitter, you will definitely miss out on some of their comments.

• No on-site analysis of data. There is no analysis of what happens with your tweets. This feature is what makes Facebook unique and it is absent on Twitter. There are other systems that can track your Twitter interaction, and this functionality will come over time.

| Social Media Channel | What it's used for | Examples of use |
|---|---|---|
| **Twitter** | • Quick and short updates (less than 140 characters).<br><br>• Often used for quick headlines from blogs, key messages from a brand and to interaction with customers.<br><br>• Customer service issues are often highlighted on Twitter - so keep an eye on it! | • Share the latest information on your range of products and services.<br><br>• Update on daily facts and figures related to your topics.<br><br>• Share customer testimonials and reviews.<br><br>• Ask for feedback on the latest blogs.<br><br>• Share the latest event for your community. |

## LinkedIn

LinkedIn is your professional profile and I think for anybody in their working life, and especially in a business life, having a good up-to-date LinkedIn profile is very useful.

Connections on LinkedIn are made by connecting people that you know. Unlike Facebook and most other Social Media networks, you must confirm that you know the people you are connected to. This is important to LinkedIn, as it shows that you know the people you are connected to and can vouch for them in a professional sense.

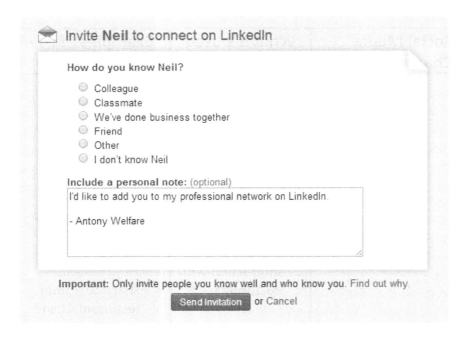

As you can see on this image, you must click "How do you know....?" to maintain connected integrity on the network.

LinkedIn is very much for job opportunities; it is your online CV, so people will approach you for job opportunities, which is normally not relevant for small business owners, but there is a group side to LinkedIn.

On LinkedIn, you have a number of groups and they are professionally related. As a business, you can use these groups for research, connections and to build a community. There are groups about authors writing this subject, understanding Social Media, or different groups where people join and, again like Facebook, can interact with each other, share ideas and just build a community.

LinkedIn is similar to Facebook, but it definitely more 'errs' to the professional side, which as a business owner, it is very useful for the professional side of what you are doing.

Building groups on LinkedIn can bring about great opportunities and the interactions can be of high quality as you grow a network of interested community members.

**Advantages of LinkedIn**

• Connect with old colleagues. You can post your CV, include all the companies you have worked for and it helps find connections from those jobs for you to connect with.

• Online, visible recommendations. You can have recommendations from people displayed on your page. Great to keep track of personal references for referrals.

• Groups. You can join groups related to your business as a way of meeting new people and building a community.

**Disadvantages of LinkedIn**

• Not user-friendly. LinkedIn does need some time to understand the way it works and how to best use it.

• Hard to make sales. Not a great site for generating leads or getting people to take action to use your services, unless you are a recruitment agency.

- You must have a real photograph. You have to use a photograph of yourself, or the site will flag you. To be fair, this is important as LinkedIn is a professional network and people should know you to connect with you.

- Less frequent usage. Users do not check their pages daily, and some people will not check it for months.

| Social Media Channel | What it's used for | Examples of use |
|---|---|---|
| **LinkedIn** | • Business networking and sharing of professional information.<br><br>• Not used extensively in marketing but used as a professional business person and as a business. | • Ensure you have a personal LinkedIn page with your history and details.<br><br>• Ensure you have a business page with your details.<br><br>• Use the page to share links to your blogs and sometimes your products. |

## YouTube

One of the best and fastest growing Social Media networks is YouTube; here is where we get more visual. The most visual Social Media network is using videos. There are a few other video sharing website, such as Vimeo, which are also very useful for businesses.

Video has grown significantly over the last few years thanks to the improvements in technology. As discussed earlier, the E-Revolution has brought about much improved networks and data transfer, alongside more powerful and more mobile technology. The world is now full on smartphones on Wi-Fi or 4G networks; this is the perfect combination to watch videos at your leisure, wherever you may be.

Videos are very important for your business. Your products and services are static items, but with a video you can tell a story much better. You can engage with your community much better, and you can add value to their lives.

### *If a picture tells a thousand words a video must tell a million words!*

It is important to know that Google owns YouTube. This means that whatever you put on to YouTube will be searched and indexed a lot higher (in the rankings) than any other video sites, because Google owns it, and obviously they want to promote it and share content.

A video by far is the best way to get your messages across to your community, but it needs to be a good video; short, snappy, to the point. When you upload your video onto YouTube, make sure you use the 'tag' function and the 'description' function to put in your keywords; this ensure that you can be found when people search for you.

YouTube is simple to join; you can use a Google account if you have one set up. Once on YouTube, go to 'My Channels' where you upload your videos. If you have more than one business, you can set up more channels with relevant videos for the differing communities.

## Advantages of using Youtube

- Fast and easy video sharing. Once you have an account, uploading and then sharing your videos happens is a few minutes. You can then share these videos to all your other Social Media networks directly from YouTube.

- Differing privacy features. You can make your video public, private or unlisted, depending on who you want to see your work.

- Quick access to various videos. The search function is powered by Google, and is therefore extremely fast and accurate in finding what you and your community are looking for.

- Safe browsing. The service is regularly monitored and ensure highest levels of safety and security for your videos.

- Easy rating and feedback system. Once you have your video uploaded, it can be easily rated, viewed and shared by your community.

- Multiple size functionality. YouTube can automatically share your video in different sizes and formats, so you can embed the video in your website or share the video on Facebook, in the right format for the platform.

- Multiple apps and browsers. YouTube has many different apps and access points, so you can easily view videos on most devices and most systems.

**Disadvantages of using YouTube**

- This is public, so anyone can see the videos you post. Your videos can be shared and sent around the world with little regulations.

- Anyone can post a video. There are issues of some videos being posted that are not correct and lack integrity.

- There could be issues of privacy invasion and copyright infringement issues if your video is taken and copied.

| Social Media Channel | What it's used for | Examples of use |
|---|---|---|
| YouTube | • Sharing video content.<br><br>• Very useful for 'how to' videos and to really show off your business. | • Post a video of you introducing your products and services.<br><br>• Film a 'how to' guide that explains how to use your services.<br><br>• Show your products being used in a real-life situation. |

## Pinterest

Pinterest is a Social Media network for the more visual users. Pinterest is perfect if you are in the creative or visual industries. Pinterest is a selection of photos and images, which is perfect if you are selling visual products and service, such as if you are advising fashion trends, or if you are an interior designer.

Pinterest is a simple concept as a social network. You literally 'pin' images that you like to 'boards' that you create. Imagine you read lots of books or you like to photograph scenery; you can set up a 'Books I love' and a 'Beautiful scenery' board. The ability to set up boards is a clever way to sort your images and photographs into logical groupings.

With Pinterest, you can 'pin' other images and photographs from most pages on the Internet. This is a powerful advantage if you want to build a visual image of you, your brand and your business.

What Pinterest does well, is to give a visual representation of you, your business and your niche. This can be searched and viewed by everybody, which means that you can build a lovely set of boards and images that represent you and your business.

Pinterest is for all businesses, but works especially well in creative industries and fashion industries. People love the ability to 'see' this person, look at the images that they like, look at what they look at and it gives them inspiration; it gives them an insight into the personality of the person in that business.

The other great benefit of Pinterest is to use it yourself as an 'inspiration' board. You can use the 'pin it' feature on your normal web browser to easily 'pin' photographs and images that you like. You can then view these later when you are writing your blog, or developing your next product; a very powerful feature for every business owner. You can also use Pinterest to keep note of ideas and images for your next blog and Social Media updates. This creates ready-made blog content for the future.

## Advantages of Pinterest

- Use it as a tool to record things that interest you and are part of your thought process when you build your product range and services, and blogs.

- Easy to save images to support your blog and Social Media networks.

- Pinterest is beneficial for visual businesses such as interior designers, fashion companies and lifestyle magazines to promote their products and inspirations.

- By creating mood boards around your different influencers or projects, you engage with your community and drive interest to your other Social Media channels where you can connect and discuss.

- Pinterest is also a great tool to use when you are planning an event and want to collate a variety of elements in one place.

- Unlike certain Social Media tools, Pinterest's early adopters appear to have been women with mainstream interests like design, fashion and travel. They are genuinely engaged and hopefully will stay interested in your products and services.

- Pinterest is both attractive to look at and easy to use.

## Disadvantages of Pinterest

- There is no easy way to connect and chat via Pinterest

- There are potential privacy concerns because Pinterest forces you to link through either your Twitter or Facebook accounts.

- Pinterest's current privacy policy is not crystal clear when it comes to what information they share with your other Social Media channels.

- Pinterest faces issues with images that are copyrighted. They face a growing backlash from media owners and users over their somewhat vague attitude to copyright. Pinterest's terms of use put the emphasis on you to make sure there are no copyright or licensing violations, so it could be you that is sued.

| Social Media Channel | What it's used for | Examples of use |
|---|---|---|
| **Pinterest** | • A channel where you 'pin' photos of products and things that you like.<br><br>• Very visual – remember a picture tells a thousand words.<br><br>• Great to showcase you and your business images. Add plenty of product photography to your boards.<br><br>• Use this channel as a visual representation of your business. | • Open a page as a person and set up a 'board' with products you like – include yours and others.<br><br>• Use the boards as 'bookmarks' for images that inspire you.<br><br>• 'Pin' images to a board and use in your blogs and on the other Social Media channels.<br><br>• Open a page as your business and share the images that inspire your brand.<br><br>• Share the images that have inspired you to write your blogs. |

## Instagram

The next social network to look at is Instagram. Instagram is owned by Facebook, which is important to understand in the context of social networking sites. For a start, this means Instagram is supported and will be here for the long term (assuming it is a viable business). It also means that you can easily integrate with Facebook and your communities. One of the issues with Pinterest is the lack of ability to connect with your community and discuss things. Facebook is the place to have discussions and Instagram can be used in a similar way to Pinterest.

Instagram is a photo image social network where you upload and share a photo or image. There are a number of 'filters' built into the apps which you use to upload the images. These range from making the photo brighter and bolder, to making them black and white. These are easy to use tools, which can help define your book and your business. You can also put text onto the message carrying the image, which makes Instagram more interactional.

As a business, it is quite hard to work out how to use Instagram at the moment, but people tend to photograph where they are, what they are doing and put comments, and it builds up again an image and an understanding of the person.

Your customers may not really look at Instagram too much, but they may see a picture of you delivering a training event. They may see a picture of your product and it may just set them off thinking that they want to know more about this person.

For me, Instagram is another method of just bringing new people into your community and your network. You could find that some people love Instagram and they use it a lot to view and share images. Not having a presence on Instagram could mean that you miss gaining these people in your community.

Recently, Instagram have brought out the functionality where you can film a very short video, about 10 seconds in length. This is a great development as it can give a quick snapshot of what you are about, what your business is about, and allow people to learn more about you.

Using Instagram is very simple and it is an easy to use Social Media network. It is gaining in popularity and I would think that your community will start to use it, so make sure you take a look at it for your book and business.

**Advantages of Instagram**

- Instagram is great, especially if you are fond of taking pictures and uploading them right away for other people to see.

- It's fast to upload on Instagram using the apps on smartphones and tablet PCs.

- Your photos can be automatically uploaded or posted on your Facebook and Twitter accounts.

- Instagram offers a lot of photo effects and filters.

- You can be updated on your friends' happenings or your friends' important announcements.

- It is a great way of making or meeting new friends.

- You can also advertise your own products if you have a business or shops. You can take a photo of your products and post it on Instagram and it can help you gain more customers.

- Your posts also live on forever. They do not disappear or get archived like old tweets.

- Connect with a targeted audience. Take advantage of the smaller community on Instagram to cultivate real brand advocates and loyal customers.

- Instagram users are passionate and active. They want to interact with you and get to know you.

- Photos immediately convey emotional responses. You can easily use your posts to evoke powerful emotions in your community in order to produce the reactions you desire.

**Disadvantages of Instagram**

- Instagram has limited features. It is simple for posting a photo and a short caption.

- Loss of copyright ownership. Instagram owns the copyright of the photograph.

- Instagram is a great place to store, caption and share photos but the fear of Facebook using Instagram to generate revenues makes photographers rethink how they use the photo sharing app.

| Social Media Channel | What it's used for | Examples of use |
|---|---|---|
| **Instagram** | • A place where you can post photos or videos.<br><br>• Choose a 'filter' to enhance its look and feel.<br><br>• Use # to categorise content.<br><br>• Search for relevant content to follow.<br><br>• Easily follow and tag thought leaders. | • Upload photos of your products and service.<br><br>• Upload photos of customers interacting with your products and services.<br><br>• Upload photos of your business at different times of the year. |

## Google+

Finally, and by no means least, we have Google+. Google+ is very much like Facebook and LinkedIn. It is Google's community or social app. Google obviously owns this which means that content on here will obviously be searched and ranked very highly in a Google search.

Again, it is about sharing; it is about establishing a community here – it is called a 'circle'. We would normally call it a community where you have a circle of friends. You can have different circles, or different communities of friends which helps segment your community. So, for example, if you have got a number of products and services, you could set up a community, or a circle, for each of them. So you can discuss and have group conversations and interactions within that circle.

Being Google, there are some cool technologies you can use. You can hold a Google 'hangout', which is video conferencing for the new world, or you can use Google messenger to keep all your messages in one place (see the next section, *Google – Your BEST friend on the Internet*)

**Advantages of Google+**

- Separates work and personal engagements with your different circles and settings.

- Google+ has an easy way of separating your work contacts and personal life contacts.

- Video chatting is a great benefit via hangouts. You can chat with your community through video, seeing them face-to-face from anywhere.

- It is interlinked with other services. All other services of Google are integrated within the social networking site.

**Disadvantages of Google+**

- Lengthy posts. There is no limit to character usage and so you can exhaustively say what you want. This causes difficulties while scanning for specific things.

- Difficult in navigation. The more people you connect to, the harder it becomes to navigate with ease.

- Not clustered. Since Google + is not as crowded as Facebook or Twitter, there is clear lack of mass that can be reached at once for marketing purposes.

| Social Media Channel | What it's used for | Examples of use |
|---|---|---|
| Google+ | • Similar to Facebook, but more recent.<br><br>• Used daily by millions of people to keep in touch, share photos and interact.<br><br>• More business focused, but still very new.<br><br>• Important to note – Google is the world's number one search engine. Posting updates and content on Google+ will mean you have a better page ranking and more visits. | • Upload product photographs and information.<br><br>• Share a paragraph about a new product and services.<br><br>• Update your page with your latest new range or downloads.<br><br>• Share your new promotions.<br><br>• Promote an event.<br><br>• Hold a hangout with your community. |

## Google – Your BEST friend on the Internet

I know this is not strictly Social Media but without sounding like Google's number one fan, I would like to introduce and show you what Google has to offer for your business.

Throughout the book, you have seen references to Google, and here I will summarise why they are so important to your business.

The first thing you need to do is to set up a Google account for your business:

https://accounts.google.com/SignUp

Simply follow the initial signing up process, as shown below. You will need a Google account to use all the free tools Google provides to help you promote and grow your store.

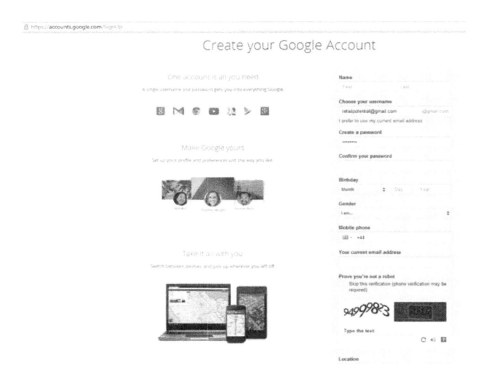

**Applications that you can access from your Google account... for your business**

*Image source: http://www.ewcertified.ca/google-for-your-business/*

**Google Web Search**

This is where most people start their internet search... including YOUR customers.

How any times do you hear, "Just Google it?"... and we all know what that now means. People search for everything on Google, and that includes the products that you sell.

A Google search is based on complex algorithms, which have been developed over tens of years. Google has one aim, and that is to give the user the exact answer they are searching for. For Google to deliver that goal, they continually develop and improve their algorithms.

It is important to realise that as an online business, you cannot outsmart Google. Gone are the days when you could type in your keyword one thousand times and you come up on the first search page. Now there is much more to it, and more to come.

### The key rules for a Google search:

- Relevance – Is your website relevant to what the user has typed into the search browser (or spoken via the speech app)?

- Credibility – Is your website credible? With lots of credible content and plenty of interaction?

- Accessibility – Is your website accessible for users and easy to navigate?

- Volume – Is there a decent volume of traffic to your website? Browsing and buying from your store?

- Links – Do you have credible links back to your website where people can share your content and like your pages?

**Google Analytics**

Google Analytics is a very useful tool for tracking and analysing your website's traffic. The level of detail overwhelms many people who use Google Analytics. (More later)

**Google AdWords**

Google's main revenue generator is its AdWords pay-per-click programme. Not all e-commerce owners want to spend money to generate traffic, but at some stage all e-commerce businesses use AdWords.

The reason so many business owners do use AdWords is because it works for them in producing a positive return on the 'ad pounds' they spend.

At the very least, you should educate yourself about AdWords and make sure you use your keywords that you developed earlier in the programme.

**Google Maps/Local Search**

Google Local Search might not be relevant for every e-commerce site, but there is a rapid shift occurring across all the major social/search web properties to emphasise the local aspect of search. You will want to develop a local strategy and stake your claim in your city or region.

The best place to start is by establishing your Google local listing. Here, you add your basic business details and it will then show up on Google Search for that location – every extra placing on Google will result in more hits to your website.

Google is testing a paid enhanced local listing service, which allows participants to create a more developed listing that displays in Google local results, and includes links to photos, videos, coupons, and other specific business information.

**Google Webmaster Tools**

Webmaster Tools gives you valuable stats about how Google views and crawls your website. You can see data, such as the most common keywords which Google associates with your pages, or the anchor text found in external links to your site.

Webmaster Tools now has a site performance section that gives data on the load time of your pages.

Some very useful information to help grow your business.

## Simple and automated ways to share content

Once you have established your Social Media profiles and pages, you need to find a good way to share content across all these networks. I will discuss this in depth in the strategy section, but for now I will cover a couple of key ways to share content.

The first way to share content is via the 'share' icons that exist on most blogs and social networking sites. You will all have read a news article or blog and seen a selection of Social Media icons which enable you to easily share this content with your network.

There are some very simple sharing icons and some more complex.

Above is a very common and simple way to share your content with your networks. All you need to do is click on the Social Media network image, log in and share the content direct with your community.

Articles and blogs often have the ability to comment and engage in conversations; this can be solely on the blog or as part of a Social Media network. You should make sure that your blog has the comment and share options, to enable your community to share your content easily.

There is a way to share content automatically, and time your content updates. This is done by using software which allows you to share. The one I use is Hootsuite and they allow you to set up all your networks in one place and share content in a timed fashion.

Using this type of software is a great way to efficiently grow your community and market your books and business. I tend to share all my content via Hootsuite and spend a few hours once or twice a month setting this up.

As you can see in the screenshot, I have three networks on the profile (Twitter, Facebook and Vimeo) and it shows my Twitter direct messages and the scheduled tweets.

You can customise all these to exactly what you want to see and in which column.

## Social Media networks and mobile devices

Social Media is something that we do in our own time and when we decide. This is a big change to old media which was 'pushed' at us. With Social Media, we are in control. As discussed in the E-Revolution chapter, the changes in technology and connectivity has given us all access to affordable mobile devices such as smartphones and tablet computers.

These new devices have allowed us to access Social Media 24/7 and on the move. All Social Media networks offer mobile apps (applications or software) which allows you to access your Social Media networks on the go.

This is a great benefit for you as a business. Time is one of our most precious resources and I do not recommend you spending hours of your time sat at your desk on Social Media networks. This will not make you money; you must write and share content, and make sure you interact with your community. Mobile and apps allow you to do this on the move and in between meetings and events.

You can also use the apps to write and develop content whilst you are on the move. You can use note apps that allow you to scribble down ideas wherever you maybe. You can use the camera app and then share the images with yourself if you have some inspiration.

Mobile use of Social Media networks is a game changer in terms of your time. We now have the ability to be connected and interacting on Social Media networks 24/7, and more importantly when we have time to spare, such as when travelling.

The quality and usability of these apps varies with the social networking platform, but they are all available and will make keeping in touch with your community much easier. They are all simple to download; just go into your app store (App Store or Play Store) and download the latest version of the networks you are using.

Log on to the profiles and you are free to use Social Media on the go. This is a great way to share live photos of your training, update your community with breaking news, or just share a cool video that you have watched recently.

# Chapter 7: The importance of blogs

## The blog basics

*What is a blog?*
*Originally, it was a type of online journal or diary,*
*often including personal comments as well as web links and*
*images. Now, a blog is the main method of communication in*
*the Social Media world.*

Blogs are very popular and they are a great, inexpensive way to connect with more customers, and help build a community.

The great thing about blogs is that people read them for fun and in their own time. Customers are becoming more jaded about advertising, but they will gladly read a blog that has some interesting things to say, and is relevant to their community.

Many large companies are using blogs to deliver a better and more personal message about their companies, products and services – and this strategy seems to be working.

In general, you will want to develop a central theme for your blog in the same way that news columnists develop a theme for their articles. This helps ensure that your blog is not too scattered and meets the needs of your community.

Next, find some places to publish your blog. There are a number of sites – both paying and free – that give bloggers a chance to publish their material.

Along with your own places for your blog, you should take advantage of the blogging system that LinkedIn created in 2014. It is called a 'post' and you can share your blogs/posts with the entire LinkedIn network. This could gain you thousands of views and interactions (there is more on this in the LinkedIn section).

Once you have a place to publish your blog, you will have to set aside some time each week to develop new content. This is key to creating a long-term and sustainable community.

When you are writing your blog:

- Write simply and clearly. Use small paragraphs and spell check before uploading.

- Use your own language. Your readers will trust what you have to say if you say it well and consistently.

- Go easy on the advertising. The idea of a blog is to give readers something fun, exciting to read and visually appealing.

- Consider writing about your day, the atmosphere your workplace has, and culture, rather than just your company. People like to get to 'know' companies and a blog is an ideal method to bring out a companies personality.

- Use images and videos. Consider many types of creative content, not just text. Blogs allow you to upload images, create links, and allow users to make comments. Your blog will have many more readers if you make your blog exciting.

## Blog marketing ideas that work...

Once you develop a blog, you will want to use the best blog marketing strategies you can to sell your products and services. However, marketing blogs are different from personal blogs, and blog marketing or advertising is very different than other forms of marketing.

In order to make your blog a powerful marketing tool, you need your customers and community to see it. That means that you will need to provide content that gets attention.

- Make your blog visually exciting. Choose an attractive background colour and provide photos or images. Develop your blog as you would a website, with the same visual appeal. Good bloggers even add video and sound to their blogs.

- There is no need to spend many hours composing artwork, but know that simple text on a white background may simply not draw as many readers as you like.

Studies suggest that 50% of online users read blogs. This means that if you can give your blog community what they want, you can be reasonably sure of having a good audience.

Ideas for content that you may want to include in your blog:

- Tips and advice. Many successful marketing blogs are much like successful customer magazines — readers tune in to read content that is useful. A computer company can offer computer tips and advice. For example, an author's blog can include daily ways to boost writing skills.

- Create interest. If your personal or business life is fascinating, then great. There are many successful marketing blogs that detail the exciting lives of company presidents who are also hobby race car drivers or skydivers. This sort of material can ensure a steady audience.

- Humanity. One of the things that blog readers are most interested to see is the face behind the company. Many blog readers like a company run by people who have similar concerns. Building humanity into your blog by detailing your company's efforts to help the community, for example, is a great way to build credibility and customer loyalty.

- Style. Many readers just love to see a gorgeous, well written blog. Plenty of marketing blogs simply provide interesting content and nice graphics, and do quite well in drawing readers and customers.

## Get more readers for your blog, get more customers

There are several ways to make your blog one of the 'hot' blogs online. Traditionally, those companies that have the largest 'star power'have had the most popular blogs, since everyone loves to read about celebrity or success.

However, many smaller companies and individuals are developing large followings on the web.

- Keep it content rich. Blogs are a great way to generate keyword rich content, especially if you update your blogs each day. In fact, for some smaller businesses, blogs make more sense than web pages. Blog software makes creating a blog almost automatic while the spiders on search engines seem to favour high-quality and regularly updated keyword-rich blogs.

- Keep keyword content high with plenty of keywords. As you write your blog entries, do try to use not only keywords having to do with your topic, but also synonyms for your keywords.

- Provide good quality and often updated content.

- Specialise and find your niche. The best way to make use of the search engine optimisation of blogs is to narrow your focus. Rather than developing a range of ideas and themes, write with one theme in mind. It will help ensure that people looking for information on your topic will always find you through a search engine.

- Join in the community. Make sure that you promote your blog by joining the blogging community. Creating a larger presence for your blog online will result in more blog readers and, possibly, more customers.
  - Add the address for your blog to email signatures and include a mention in any email newsletter you have to let readers know about your blog.
  - Mention your blog on appropriate forums and groups, especially in your LinkedIn groups.

- Allow for readers' commentary on your blog. Many online blog publishing programmes already allow this. If your readers can post their comments and read the comments of other readers, they are more likely to return to your blog regularly, and so keep your company name in mind.

- Make your blog searchable through your interests. Many blog programmes allow you to create a user profile, which allows readers to search for you and your blog by interest topic and locations, in many cases. Do not overlook this simple way to draw readers. Simply fill out your profile, taking care to use many 'interests' to attract more readers and browsers.

# Chapter 8: Build a Community

## Build a community

The aim of Social Media for businesses is to build a community – to build a following of people that want to interact and connect with you. You want to build an engaged community who want to listen to your message and connect with you on a frequent basis via Social Media.

With Social Media, you can build your own community of people who want to follow you, like you, love you and connect with you. The different Social Media channels call these different things, but it is all about gaining engaged followers.

You want your community to 'like' your comments – to say, "Yes I like this, this is an interesting blog," or, "This is an interesting tweet," and then you want your community to start sharing the content or messages. You want your community to say, "That is a great piece of information, I will share that with my friends and my community". From this share or 'like', you will grow your community.

The power of one person in your community 'liking' and sharing content comes from the fact that we trust each other, in terms of friends. If our friends like, share or tweet something, we want to know about it and we are interested in what they have to say.

Within a social network, if we are connected and you tell me that this is a great book or that there is this great service or great product, I will look at it. I will also Google it, and I will go on Facebook, look at the page or have a look at the tweets. If you have recommended it, there has got to be something about it that could be of interest to me.

With all these different Social Media channels in existence, the key is to use the ones your customers use, and engage with your community on these Social Media networks. Do not just ask them to share. Do not just ask them to like your content. Ask them to talk about it, and ask you questions. Ask open questions, post a blog or post an update and ask, "What are your thoughts? Do you agree that this is the future? Do you agree that this should happen?"

Engage with your customers, because the more community, the more discussions you have, and the more powerful and the better your product and services become. With all this information, you can change your products and services, and update them to fit exactly what your customers want. Remember, the power of Social Media is worldwide.

Once you build your community, you may have customers interacting with you from different continents, where their experience will be so different from your local communities. This can add a completely different dimension to your products and services, and you can use this information to enrich the lives of your community.

The key is to build the community, get people to like your content, get them to share it and, most importantly, engage with them and make it interactive and fun. Upload photos and images, make it a fun time so that they want to go and look at your Facebook page or join your LinkedIn group. Make them want to read your tweets and become excited about visiting your YouTube channel.

Most importantly, build yourself a community and network with people who are your supporters, your fans who want to be part of your community. They will be your strongest voice and your biggest critics as you and your business grows.

To grow a successful community, you need good content and a supportive outlook on life. The next few sections talk you through how to grow and build a successful and loving community.

## Follow and be followed

When you start building your networks, you will have to build your followers. To do this, at the start I advise you to follow the rule of "Follow and be followed". This means that if you follow a person, especially on the feeder networks such as Twitter and Pinterest, people will follow you back.

Develop a strategy to follow people who you know are likely to be of influence and be a part of your community:

- Your industry leaders

- Celebrities in your industry

- People who blog in your industry

- People who have large social networks in your industry

- People you know

- Customers you have worked for

- Colleagues you have worked with

- Clients you have served

- Your business network

Follow as many relevant people as you can. By doing this, they are likely to follow you back and will help build your community.

## Engage with who YOU follow

When you start following people, make sure you become engaged in what they are saying and what they are talking about. One of the best, and quickest, ways to gain a following for your book is to comment on other people's blogs and Social Media networks.

I do not mean advertise your products and services on their blogs, but engage in the topic of discussion that they have posted on. Share your opinion and your expertise. If people like what you are saying, they will follow you.

Actively join groups on LinkedIn, follow people on Twitter and follow pages on Facebook. By becoming an active participant in relevant groups and on relevant pages, you will become noticed for your opinions and content.

*The more you share and comment,*
*the more you will gain a following and build a community.*

## Make them love you

Building a community of people that like you is great, but building a community of people who love you is what you want to strive for.

*If you have a community that loves you,*
*they will be all you need to grow and develop.*

It takes time for people to love you, just like in physical life, but the success from this effort will be worth it. To get people to love you takes a lot of understanding of your customer and what they need. To have a person love you, you have to understand what they are looking for in your community and deliver that.

Whatever information they are looking for, you must deliver:

• Frequently. Make sure you interact with your community on a daily basis and keep it interesting and exciting.

• Consistently. Regularly update your community with the same style and quality of content from your products and your services.

• Unequivocally. Share your content without expecting a return on that content. A return will come overtime with your entire package.

• With abundance. Give, give, give. Share as much content as you can.

• And with a high level of respect and quality.

Delivering content and information this way will help you build a community that loves you. Remember to respect the fact that your community have chosen to give their own time to you; treat them like VIPs and give them the content and interaction they love.

## Engage and enrich your community

To enable your community to love your content, you need to give something back to them and improve their lives in some way.

The first part of this is to engage with your communities. You need to start conversations and you need to join conversations. Commenting on another blog, or your own blog, with your thoughts and feelings will engage your community, and allow them to join in with the conversation.

When you comment on other blogs and other people's Social Media channels, be fair, honest and engaging. You are building a community that loves you and you must respect other people's opinions and other people's views. That does not mean you do not comment; it means you comment and engage in conversation with respect.

The best way to engage with your own community is to enrich their lives. Add and share content that helps them improve their lives or understand their lives better. Good quality content that enriches lives can be shared and used by your community. The effect of this will help grow your community and make them love you even more.

## Give, Share, Support – Principles for great communities

Sharing good quality content will enrich your community and you can follow these three principles for good content:

1. Give. Give lots of content; blogs, tweets, videos, images etc. Make sure you are always giving to your community lots of relevant and great content.

2. Share. Once you have given lots of content, make sure you share this content. Use the Social Media networks to share your content with other communities, other people who may be interested in your message, and your community

3. Support. Giving and sharing lots of content will lead to lots of engagement with your community. This engagement will not only be in the forms of sharing and liking, but also people commenting and having a conversation. Make sure you are supporting your community and having conversations with them and answering their questions and concerns.

Giving and sharing alone do not make a great community; conversations and support make the community. Ensure you support and have conversations with your community.

## Follow, Like, Love – The ultimate aim of Social Media

The ultimate aim of Social Media is to grow and cultivate an engaged community.

I have developed a three-step model in order to help you build the community that you want.

1. Follow. Help your communities to follow you. This is done by giving, sharing and supporting great content and great conversations.

2. Like. Once they are following you, get your communities to like you; give them a reason to say, "I like this post/image/video." Provide life-enriching content for your community.

3. Love. Now that your community follows you and likes you, you want to help them love you. If you have people that love you in your communities, they become your ambassadors and your most influential supporters. Help your community to love you by helping them engage with you, not just liking and sharing, but actively commenting and interacting with other members in your community. You want to make your community members proud of the community and happy to say that they love this particular community.

The next chapter will give you the strategy and techniques you need to build your community around your business.

# Chapter 9: Plan your Social Media strategy

## You must have a strategy and plan Social Media

### *Failure to plan, is planning to fail*
### *Have a plan, have a strategy*

As with anything in business, you need to have a plan, and Social Media is exactly the same. A lot of people make the mistake of opening a Facebook account, setting up a LinkedIn profile, and setting up a Twitter account, then they write a few tweets, share a few videos and then sit there and wonder why nothing is happening. Why is nobody interacting? Why are people not visiting my website? Why is there no downloads of my products? Why are people not coming to see me? It is because there is no plan.

You need to look at what you are trying to do and piece together the process to get there. It is quite a long journey in terms of how to get from a number of Social Media sites to a product, a service or something that your customer buys and interacts with.

## Social Media Strategy for Business

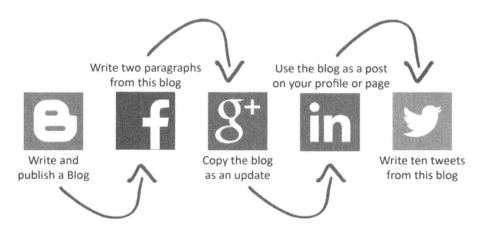

Write two paragraphs from this blog

Use the blog as a post on your profile or page

Write and publish a Blog

Copy the blog as an update

Write ten tweets from this blog

**The Social Media for Business Strategy**

1. Start with your blog. Your blog is the most important item of content. You should concentrate on writing this first and then use this as the basis for all the other Social Media channels.

2. Share your blog. Communicate it via all your Social Media channels. Make sure you have all the share buttons on your blog to allow for easy sharing by your community.

3. Links to your website. Make sure you have links to your products and images on the blog article; you want your customers to buy your products and services ultimately.

4. Take the key points from your blog and write a paragraph for Facebook/Google+/LinkedIn.

5. Link this update to your blog page, so that when the customer reads, and likes the paragraph, they can read the full blog.

6. Write impactful and enticing content. Make sure your content is interesting and  to ensure your Facebook/Google+ customer reads it and clicks through.

7. Take 10 key sentences from the blog and use them for Twitter. Once you have written your blog article and paragraph update, you should take the 10 key messages (of less than 140 characters) and use these to entice your customers on Twitter to click through and read the blog.  Make sure you add the link to your tweets.

8. Use images. "An image is worth a thousand words".  Make sure you have images in every blog, even if the blog is for information only.  Include pictures of your book and other images you have.

9. Use videos. If you have a great story and want to share a message over a wider audience, keep it short and to the point.

## Social Media marketing plan for Businesses

To help you set your Social Media marketing plan for your business, I have developed a step-by-step plan. This can be downloaded for free as an excel spreadsheet from www.retailpotential.com to enable you to use it immediately.

| Step | Action | Details |
|------|--------|---------|
|      |        |         |
| 1 | Know your customer | Understand what your customers are talking about in relation to your business. Translate these words and phrases to the Social Media world. |
|   |                    | What keywords do they use? What words would they search for? Do they prefer words or images? |
|   |                    |         |
| 2 | Know which Social Media channels your customers use | Understand which channels your customers use in the Social Media world – blogs, email, Twitter, Facebook, LinkedIn, YouTube, Pinterest etc. |
|   |                    | Which Social Media channels do they use? What subject lines do they like? What times do they use Social Media? Do they comment on blogs? Do they share content? |
|   |                    |         |
| 3 | Test, Monitor, Change (TMC) | Test the different Social Media channels and different words – this takes time and needs to happen often to refine your message to your community. |

| | | |
|---|---|---|
| 4 | Target your customers | Once you have trialled a few Social Media channels and words, start to target your customers using this knowledge. |
| | | Look at different areas, interests, followers, groups etc. |
| 5 | Co-ordinate a 'theme' | Develop a Social Media theme for each month. |
| | | Co-ordinate all the Social Media channels starting with a blog – is this period's theme about information? Events? History? |
| 6 | Writing Style | Write in the style firstly for your customer and secondly for the channel. |
| | | Your writing style is a reflection of your brand. |
| 7 | KEEP – Test, Monitor, Change (TMC) | Test the different channels and different words. |
| | | Change the way you write and the channels. |
| | | It takes a few months to get the right blend - keep TMC. |
| 8 | Be confident with what you produce | Be confident with your content – people will choose to follow, like and sign up to your newsletter. |
| | | They WANT to know about you, your brand and your products. |

| | | |
|---|---|---|
| 9 | Make every detail count | Remember the detail – ensure all your details are correct. |
| | | From the spelling and tags to the picture quality and positioning, get it right. |
| 10 | Use images | People love images, and images speak "a thousand words" – make your blog and newsletter interesting. |
| | | Post on Facebook and Twitter an image and some text. Make it exciting and interesting; you want your customer to click the link. |
| 11 | Use # and @ on Twitter | Use relevant # (hashtags) and @ (people) to ensure your tweets reach the target audience. |
| | | Try different # and test the response. |
| | | Use the # of the day and trending topics on Twitter. |
| 12 | Time your events. | There are lots of events every day. Link in with them if your product works with them e.g. horse racing, Olympics, motorsport, football matches, etc. |
| | | People search and talk about events; be part of their conversation. |

| 13 | Measure and respond. | Measure your success. At the start of the process, note your followers, email database size, 'Likes' on Facebook etc. |
|---|---|---|
| | | Your success in Social Media is measured by the growth of your audience, as well as sales, traffic and conversion. |

## Social Media Strategy for Businesses

To bring this all together, I want to share a Social Media model with you that you can use to market your business. This model takes all your previous testing from the plan and sets up an action plan for implementation of a successful Social Media strategy for your business.

I start the plan with a newsletter or blog, which is meant for your email database. If you do not have one (read the section on email marketing to learn why you should have one), just start with the blog and ignore the newsletter section.

---

The strategy:

1.  Start with developing the overall theme.

2.  Write the basics of the theme .

3.  Write the blog or newsletter first, whichever is the biggest item.

4.  Once the main item is written, develop the Facebook updates and then the tweets.

5.  If you have a video, link this to the blog and newsletter.

6.  Set up the sending of all the channels and make sure they are all timed as per the guidelines.

7.  Have a clear 'Call to Action' i.e. visit the website, sign up or purchase etc. Make it consistent.

---

The timings of when you share Social Media updates are important. Here are some suggested ideas:

| Social Media | Timings to be sent out | Guideline |
|---|---|---|
| **Blog** | **Blog** | |
| 3x a month | 12.30 p.m. | Share a story about your new product range or services. |
| | | Focus on one part of the range for the story behind the range. |
| | | Make that into an interesting blog. |
| | | Allow the blog to be interactive, and ask for comments and opinions. |
| **Newsletter** | **Newsletter** | |
| 3x a month | 12.30 p.m. or | Use the blog and take one interesting paragraph that explains the majority story of the blog. |
| | 6.30 p.m. to 7.30 p.m. | Add images to the newsletter. |
| | | Add links to your videos and Social Media pages. |
| **Facebook** | **Facebook** | |
| 1 to 3 per day | 12.30 p.m. 6.30 p.m. | Key content from the blog. |
| | In the evenings | Share the images and add the link to the blog. |
| | | Share the main messages and link to the blog. |

| Twitter | Twitter | |
|---------|---------|--|
| 5 to 10 per day | 8.30 a.m. | Key content from the blog. |
| | 12.30 p.m. | Share the images and add the link to the blog. |
| | 6.30 p.m. | Share the main messages and link to the blog. |
| | to | Keep it very short and attention grabbing. |
| | 10.30 p.m. | |
| **YouTube** | **YouTube** | |
| 1 video per month | | Linked to blog and themed as per the plan for that month. |
| | | Keep the intro interesting. |
| | | Use the keywords that you are using on all the other Social Media networks. |

Once you have set up your Social Media strategy, you will need to monitor the timings to see which of your content is being viewed and interacted with. You may find that your community interact in the evenings, or you may find they interact in the daytime or weekends. Try lots of different times to find which is best for your content and your community.

# Key points for your Social Media content:

## Remember:

### Blogs
- Customers choose to visit the blog; this needs to be more in depth

- Make the story a couple of paragraphs

- This should reflect the true heart of the brand

### Newsletters
- This is the key medium we have to drive interest, visits and sales

- Must be informative and easy to read

- Maximum of five lines per story

### Facebook
- The purpose of Facebook is to get quick stories and comments to start a discussion

- Good examples reference the blog or video and ask what your followers think and want

### Twitter
- Very quick one-liners linked to the theme or real-life events

- Remember your keywords and #

### YouTube
- Use great tags to relate the content and bring together the theme

# Chapter 10: Measure and improve your Social Media strategy

## What gets measured gets managed?

As with any good plan, you need to have some measurements. Whatever you do in life, you should measure and we have all heard the saying:

*"What gets measured gets managed"*

This statement is absolutely true in life, in business and the same with Social Media. You need to set yourself targets. When you are looking at Facebook, blogs, and when you are looking at engaging with your community, you need to set yourself targets. A part of strategic planning is to decide what the targets should be and how you are going to achieve them.

To help you measure your progress in Social Media, there are a couple of ways that you can measure your Social Media progress from an external point of view, which will really help you on the journey. One of these is called Klout.

It is a Social Media measuring tool, and their philosophy is "Be Known For What You Love". Basically, they are saying that if you want to talk about and be an expert in this topic, we will help you measure to see if you are achieving what you want to be.

It is a very simple process in essence. Sign up to their website, add your LinkedIn, Facebook, and Twitter accounts, and they will then measure your Social Media networks, and every day you will have an updated 'Klout score' which is measured from 0 to 100.

Anything above 30 or so is good. Anything above 60 is very good. Anything above 70 is exceptional. Barack Obama and Justin Bieber are around about 99 and, bearing in mind they have millions and millions of followers, they are at the top of the Klout scale due to their massive Social Media following across the world.

You should not join Klout to expect to be at 100; you will not be. It is just not possible for small businesses, even large businesses, to be near the top. But what you need to do is measure your own progress. When you join, Klout will measure you, and for the first few days it will be up and down as it is measuring all your different Social Media sites, but then you will start to see a steady pattern.

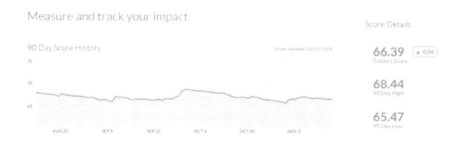

For example, when you join and you are at a Klout score of 21, you would target a growth in six weeks to a score you want to be at – let's say 23. You need to work out, "How am I going to get there?"

You can do this by looking at your Klout score breakdown and see which channel is giving you the best score. Have a look at whether it is your Facebook, Twitter, or Pinterest. Whichever of your Social Media sites are adding the most to your score tells you where your customers are and where you are influencing them.

## Network Contribution

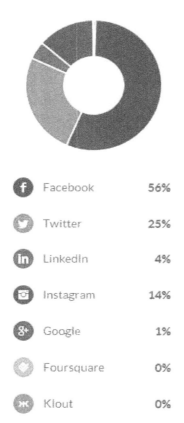

| | | |
|---|---|---|
| Facebook | 56% |
| Twitter | 25% |
| LinkedIn | 4% |
| Instagram | 14% |
| Google | 1% |
| Foursquare | 0% |
| Klout | 0% |

For example, look at the above example, where my Klout score is 56% from Facebook. From this information, I know that my Social Media impact is driven a lot by Facebook and the other ones are less important. This allows me to focus on the quality of the keywords and making great content for Facebook. The other Social Media networks obviously do change over time and you need to monitor this.

You might develop a new product or service, and you might do lots of videos and all of a sudden your YouTube is measured at 50% of your score; this information helps you know where you are progressing.

You can also, if you need to, benchmark yourself against other people in your industry, but bear in mind they could be using Social Media for years or they could be at the start.

Do not worry too much at the start about where your score is relative to other people. Worry about where it starts and what you want to get to, and whatever you do, do not expect to go from 20 to 30 quickly. That will take three months minimum, probably six to twelve months. It is a long process of building up credibility, building up followers, but all of the time you are adding value to your community.

## Social Media Trackers

The second way to measure your Social Media progress is by using my own Social Media Growth Tracker and Social Media Engagement Tracker.

Remember, the goal of Social Media is to build an community and to build an engaged community. You therefore need to track two statistics:

1.  Number of followers or page likes (Social Media Growth Tracker)

2.  Number of 'engagements' i.e. likes, shares and comments (Social Media Engagement Tracker)

## Social Media Growth Tracker

| Social Media Growth Tracker | Month 1 | Month 2 | Month 3 |
|---|---|---|---|
| Newsletter | | | |
| Subscribers | 100 | 110 | 125 |
| Blog | | | |
| Subscribers | 50 | 54 | 65 |
| Facebook | | | |
| Page Likes | 205 | 247 | 350 |
| Twitter | | | |
| Followers | 214 | 250 | 321 |
| YouTube | | | |
| Channel Likes | 5 | 8 | 20 |
| LinkedIn | | | |
| Friends | 50 | 56 | 62 |
| Google+ | | | |
| Page Likes | 10 | 17 | 32 |
| Instagram | | | |
| Followers | 50 | 62 | 75 |
| Pinterest | | | |
| Followers | 10 | 12 | 15 |

Copyright Retail Potential Ltd 2014

**Notes:**

- We assume you are using Facebook as a page for business, not your own personal profile.
- We do not suggest you grow friends on LinkedIn; just share your messages and grow your presence.
- You will not need to use all the channels.
- Growth is not necessarily an indication of engagement.

# Social Engagement Management Tracker

| Social Media Management | Month 1 | Month 2 | Month 3 |
|---|---|---|---|
| **Newsletter** | | | |
| Opens | | | |
| Click Throughs | | | |
| **Blog** | | | |
| Comments | | | |
| Shares | | | |
| **Facebook** | | | |
| Likes | | | |
| Shares | | | |
| Comments | | | |
| **Twitter** | | | |
| Retweets | | | |
| Favourites | | | |
| Replies/Direct Messages | | | |
| **YouTube** | | | |
| Video Likes | | | |
| Video Shares | | | |
| Video Comments | | | |
| **LinkedIn** | | | |
| Group Likes | | | |
| Content Likes | | | |
| Content Comments | | | |
| **Google+** | | | |
| Likes | | | |
| Shares | | | |
| Comments | | | |

| Instagram | | | |
|---|---|---|---|
| Favourites | | | |
| Comments | | | |
| Direct Messages | | | |
| Pinterest | | | |
| Pin Likes | | | |
| Pin Shares | | | |
| Pin Comments | | | |

Copyright Retail Potential Ltd 2014

**Notes:**
• Comments are stronger signs of engagement than likes and shares.

Monitoring your Social Media engagement tracker will show you how your community is becoming more and more engaged. This is the best measure of your Social Media success and something you can gain a lot of information from.

Analyse which of the channels is gaining the most engagement and review the posts and content that you have been posting:

• Is there a theme in the engaging content?
• Is it a certain style?
• Are there lots of images?
• Is the content controversial?
• Are you posting the content at a certain time of day?
• Is there a certain group of people within your community who are more engaged?

For all of the trackers, find out which is driving the growth and see if you can understand why.

Even if you do not know why, if it is working, keep doing it. I always say:

**If it is not broken, do not fix it**

## Social Media engagement, not social reach

Many people talk about the concept of social reach when discussing Social Media. Exactly what this means has never been fully explained, but I understand this in a more practical way.

For me, the social reach of you, your business can be easily measured via the statistics on your social networks. As I have just taken you through, we have developed two models to track your social engagement, which I believe is more important than your reach.

For me, social reach is about volume, whereas Social Media engagement is about quality. In my experience, businesses with high Social Media engagement scores have much better success rates than those with a large but unengaged network.

Social Media success is based on engagement of your community with quality and consistent content. A large unengaged network is nowhere near as valuable as a small and highly engaged network.

Make it your goal to have a high quality and highly engaged network, rather than a large unengaged network.

*Concentrating on engagement will grow your community and make your business more likely to succeed.*

## TMC (Test, Monitor, Change)

Once you have started on the journey with Social Media, you have developed a strategic plan, you are starting to look at what is working, you are updating your Facebook, you are chatting in groups on LinkedIn, and you are uploading some YouTube videos, you will then need to adopt a monitoring model and change model.

I use the TMC model as my model to monitor and change what is happening.

Firstly, you have to test your ideas; test different ways of blogging different words, different content, different images, on the different social networks and monitor them to see what happens.

Once you have started testing ideas, you need to monitor them. You could use hits on your website, likes on your Social Media accounts etc. There are many different measures; use the measuring tools I discussed previously as a beginning.

You should get into the habit and continue this on your journey. Test something out, measure it and then make the changes necessary.

The TMC model (test, monitor, change) is very much a working model, because Social Media will evolve, your business evolves, your speaking evolves, your books evolve and you need to evolve all the time.

Make sure you test something out; do not be afraid of testing something new, but monitor what happens.

Measure the impact and then change your actions as a result of what you've learnt from doing that process.

Throughout the book, we look at testing new ideas and plans, which become actions that we need to implement.

***Business, and life, is an ongoing and ever changing process which means we must continually innovate and change.***

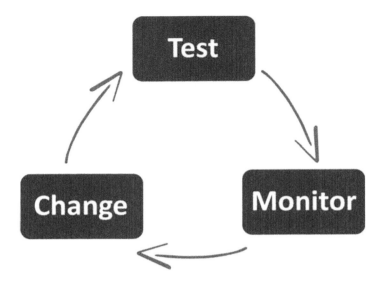

**Test**

Test the idea, action or plan – make it happen and implement the action

**Monitor**

As soon as you have implemented the action – monitor it;
- What did you think would happen?
- What is happening?
- Are good things happening?
- Are results changing?

Measure the impact of the change with real statistics from your website and business.

**Change**

Based on the results from the test and what you are have seen during the monitoring period, you are now able to change the initial plan and implement a new action.

# Chapter 11: Social Media and traditional marketing

## Social Media and email marketing

How does Social Media and email marketing work together? Your email marketing is just an extension of your blog; you put your most important content on to your blog and the same on to your email, and just keep your community happy that way.

Lots of people talk about and ask questions about email marketing and Social Media, because they are similar and they use the same process. In both cases, what you are doing is building an audience, building a community and engaging with them and communicating with them. Social Media and email marketing both do that.

The main difference is that email marketing is a lot more one-sided; it is a lot more you sharing your message. Very few people would email you back and say, "I do not agree/ I do agree; could you tell me more?" Social Media is where the interaction happens.

So, how do you use and integrate the Social Media and email marketing strategy? You should always try to build an email database, because whatever the statistics are, people still read emails. We all go on our phone and we look at our emails. We all go to the desktop, or the laptop, and we open the email programme.

Email is still an integral part of our life. I am not sure whether it is going to grow, or shrink, but I believe email marketing will get a lot more personalised, and a lot more important in terms of a smaller number of email users, with more targeted content.

With that in mind, with Social Media you can target; you can build small communities and people choose to join these. With email marketing, you are pushing a message and it needs to become more personalised to the customer.

If you have an enriched email marketing database, this is a very powerful companion to Social Media where you could email the people who live in this area, the people who like this, the people who shop in this area etc. If you can segment your email, you can give them a lot more targeted information.

An interesting development in 2014 is when Facebook now allowed you to integrate your email database with their database; this will tell you who your customers are and what they are likely to react to. It is very much on their advertising side, so you need to pay for this, but it can enrich the experience for your community and for growing the community in which you are trying to grow.

One of the benefits of email marketing, in terms of gathering the information, is you can actually build lists specifically from a campaign that you have written, a marketing campaign. For example, if you have written a blog about the E-Revolution and you have asked people to sign up to get videos, downloads, etc., they would sign up to your email list under the list 'E-Revolution' and you know that those people within your list are specifically interested in the E-Revolution.

This is helpful when you are marketing to them specifically about this subject. This is a great example of a joined up strategy where everything links and Social Media cross-promotes with your email database.

When you are signing people up to an email list, you are pushing information to them, they are not choosing to read it as they would on Social Media. You need to make sure that the reason they have signed up is the reason you have emailed them. If they signed up for information on the E-Revolution, do not send them information on how to buy a banana at the supermarket because they are probably not interested in that.

If you do not use the lists correctly, your subscribers will unsubscribe. They will leave your list and all the hard work you went to, to get them to join your list, has disappeared because they have just clicked the box that says unsubscribe and that is it; you have lost them forever. Making sure you communicate with them for the reason they ask to be communicated to is very important.

## Social Media and PR

When you launch a new service, set up, renew or refresh a business, or develop a new product range, you need to plan a launch campaign and PR plan to capitalise on the opportunity to gain 'free PR' and make sure you get off to the best start you possibly can.

PR (public relations) is very different from advertising and is the process by which you approach the press (TV, radio, newspapers, magazines, bloggers, articles etc.) to write an article about your business or services.

Good PR is being able to deliver an interesting story to the readers of the media. All journalists need interesting stories to engage their readers on a regular basis, so any great news story is beneficial to them and their readers.

In my opinion, the boundary between Social Media and PR has blurred significantly. We are now able to write our own PR stories and share them for free across blogs and Social Media networks.

Gone are the days when you had to contact a PR agency who would charge you to write your story and distribute it. You now have the power. Does this mean that there is no need for a PR agency? I believe there is a place for a PR agency, but they must understand and be experts in Social Media as well as traditional PR.

There are two major benefits of using a PR company:

1. They have an understanding of the different styles of writing that work for certain types of media. They understand and use the best techniques for online and offline PR, which is something that you will not have expert knowledge of.

2. They have a 'black book' of contacts. With Social Media, it is significantly easier to contact and interact with thought leaders and influencers. This does take time, but it is completely possible to do this yourself. Where a PR expert can add value is by having

a list of contacts, both online and offline, who they can contact and market your business and your book to. Personal contact and personal connection is still the way that the best business deals are done.

Overall, I believe that a good PR expert, who is very aware and uses Social Media, can be an asset to your business. They can offer the outside view on your business, and can offer the expert advice and knowledge when you need it.

## Social Media and "print"

Social Media Vs "old school print" is one of the hot topics. Should you use the print media world anymore, or should it all be online? I have a lot of experience of both media channels over the years, and I believe that print is not dead and still has some uses.

I would not suggest that print is the first place to market your business. The value of print has diminished significantly as the E-Revolution has grown and Social Media has taken hold. Print can have its uses for specific and co-ordinated marketing.

The best example I can use is for one of my clients, SmartWeave Shirts. This a company that has invented a shirt that does not show sweat patches, and yet is 100% cotton and a luxury quality shirt.

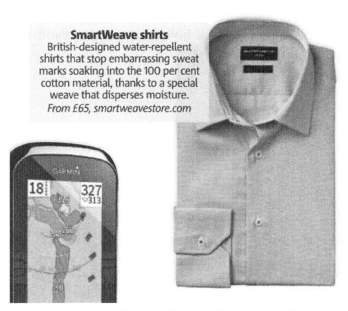

**SmartWeave shirts**
British-designed water-repellent shirts that stop embarrassing sweat marks soaking into the 100 per cent cotton material, thanks to a special weave that disperses moisture.
*From £65, smartweavestore.com*

Amongst other markets, the product is of great use for men who travel to work on the London Underground. Anybody who has travelled on the Underground in a typical British summer will know that it gets hot and sweaty down there. Even in a British winter, the deeper tubes are still hot, and the transition from cold outside to hot inside makes people sweat.

On the Tube in rush hour, you are normally standing in a very crowded carriage and people are holding on to the poles on the roof of the carriage. This shows to everybody on that carriage the sight of an armpit!  Not a pretty sight at the best of times, but in the heat it is a very unpleasant start to your day.

SmartWeave knew this fact, and they also know that when you are standing on a busy Tube, you often cannot read a book or newspaper, so you have to look at the adverts.  Bingo – you are stood on a sweaty Tube reading a print advert about a no-sweat shirt.

This was then combined with adverts in the London free newspapers, and backed up via Social Media campaigns. This total coordination of print and Social Media meant a very successful campaign for the company.

I am not suggesting we all use print for our businesses, but in certain circumstances, and as part of a holistic marketing campaign, it can add significant value to a business.

## Is Social Media the future of marketing?

I have worked with a number of companies over the last few years and seen the world of Social Media affect them in different ways. The biggest effect has been the 'blurring' of PR and Social Media. I am convinced the PR as we knew it has completely died. Social Media, with a smaller proportion of the old-style PR, is the new world model.

We can now tweet and update our Social Media networks with our PR stories a lot quicker than using a newsfeed or a newspaper. The world of Social Media is instant and needs no waiting time.

This speed of news to market is, of course, a big concern for companies. You must make sure that you word your message correctly before they are sent into the Social Media world. Once they are there, they cannot be deleted.

The marketing world and PR world have always been in line, and Social Media has meant that marketing has had to become more Social Media friendly. Gone are the days of endless planning of an advert; with Social Media networks, you have to be short and to the point.

Social Media networks have become the new media platforms. Newspapers and TV are in significant decline. The world of digital marketing has also seen a massive shift to more social networks. The world of paid-for advertising exists and is thriving, but a significant proportion of this is now moving to Social Media networks.

Social Media networks will continue to grow, and with that the marketing opportunities will grow. The future of marketing is still a balance between offline, digital and Social Media networks.

The stronger marketing opportunities will be via Social Media networks. As they understand more about their members (your communities), there will be better and more personalised information available. This is gold for any business owner that has a product and service for a niche. Using Social Media networks, you are able to define that community and sell more of your products and services easily via the Social Media networks.

# Chapter 12: What are the risks when using Social Media?

## What are the biggest risks with Social Media?

When you start to work in any way online, you have to be aware of the new world of risks and issues. The E-Revolution has changed our world forever and brought in some amazing changes and opportunities. Social Media is one of the biggest changes, and as this book discusses, there are so many benefits and improvements to lives and the world from this revolution.

As you start to establish your Social Media presence and you open your different Social Media profiles and different pages, you do have to think about the risks and the security and privacy around all the new world. You now need to think logically and look after your online and Social Media personas.

Social Media is the same as life – when you leave your house, you lock the doors, you check that the windows are shut, you turn off the gas etc. You naturally take precautions. We all live in the world, the real world, and things happen, bad things happen, and good things happen.

In Social Media, the same rules apply. Lots of people use the risks as an excuse not to open a Facebook page, or any other Social Media profile. That is your choice, but as a business, you will be out of business; you won't survive.

We know, from this book, that you have to be online, you have to have Social Media profiles, but what you need to do is to manage the risk.

**Main Risks:**

- Not everything you read is real
  - There are no rules and laws regarding what you can post, write and share online. There are guidelines by the network, but there is nothing to stop people posting what they want. This causes a problem for anybody reading Social Media and content online – how do you know the content is real?

- Fake profiles exist
  - The reality on Social Media is that you can be anyone you want to be. There are no checks for authenticity when you create a profile; you just need an email address. This can cause big issues when you accept people from a fake profile and interact with them.

- People can have different personas
  - With most social networks, you can open as many profiles as you wish. All you need is a different email address. This can be used for legitimate reasons, such as having a profile for different areas of your business or different books you have written, but it can also be used for the wrong reasons.

- What you post is a permanent record
  - This is very important. Once you have posted something to a Social Media network, there is a permanent record of that and it cannot be easily removed. There is a new law allowing you to ask search engines to remove articles, posts etc., but once you post something, it can be shared and copied onto many different channels and Social Media networks.

- Identity theft exists online
  - Unfortunately, this does exist online. People can 'steal' your online identity and pretend to be you or your business.

- Emails often have links to viruses, as do posts and links on Social Media
  - Spam and viruses are shared on Social Media, the same as they are via email. In messages, posts, updates etc., the spammers ask you to click a link that takes you outside the Social Media network and you then get hit with the virus or spam.

- People broadcast 'factless facts'; they are often not checked before they are posted and shared
  - On Social Media, it is very easy to share and like posts and comments. This means that people can often share an image or update that is factually incorrect; they do not research the link before they share. This is happening often with news stories that are made up in the first place.

- People 'buy' likes, views and friends
  - Social Media networks are often rated by the number of likes, shares, views or comments etc. This rating is seen as an important measure of your reach on Social Media. If a person wants to be seen as more popular or more credible that they are, they can buy likes from people who will go online and like, share, view etc. These are entirely fake and the networks are clamping down on these and starting to remove profiles with fake likes.

## How do you mitigate risks on Social Media?

### Manage your friends and people connecting with you

The first thing you do when you are setting up these profiles, especially with Facebook, is to only friend people you know or you know are trustworthy. Do not friend random people, do not accept invites from random people. You would not in your own physical world, you would not in your business world, so think logically, and apply the same common sense.

If somebody is trying to sell you something, if somebody is trying to friend you and you have no idea who they are and whether they are part of your network, do not accept it.

*Only accept and allow people into your space,*
*who you want to know your message and be connected to.*

### Own the profiles on each channel

The overall strategy for Social Media is to own each of the profiles on the eight main social networks I have talked about; your Facebook, your Twitter, your blogs, etc.

The reason to do this, apart from because it is the best way to use Social Media and market yourself, is that when somebody searches for you, especially your customers, you will be in the first few search results for your name. This means that if somebody does steal your identity, on a Social Media network, it is OK because all your other networks which are about you, what you do, how you work etc. will still be showing what you want. The hijacked profile will then look out of place and you can then get this deleted.

Anybody looking at your social networks will see that the hijacked profile is not you; they will see that it is somebody else because of the language.

I personally have never experienced any of this happening, but I have all my profiles up-to-date and in my name to prevent issues in the future.

**Look after your passwords**

This is simple. Keep an eye on your passwords; do not share your passwords, and don't make them too easy.  If you have a team, make sure that your team do not share passwords.

**Keep in control of what is posted on your Social Media platforms**

Keep control of everything that is posted on the Social Media platforms and keep your presence regularly updated. You should always be posting in 'your language' and 'your style'.  By doing this, if anything untoward happens, and your identity gets stolen on one of these networks, then you can easily report it to the network, close it down and restart.

## What are the biggest risks with Social Media, and the solutions?

We have already covered the main risks on Social Media networks, but now I would like to help you mitigate these risks:

- Not everything you read is real
  - ○ The easiest way to check what is real content and what is rubbish is to cross reference the content and look for reputable sources. Online, there are many reputable news sites, bloggers, companies, authors etc., and referencing information across platforms and across users will verify if it is real or fake.

- Fake profiles exist
  - ○ As with all these issues, use your common sense and look at the details of the profile and see if anything is not looking correct. A good profile will be fully completed and the information will be cross referenced with other networks, giving a fully-rounded view of the real owner of the profile.

- People can have different personas
  - ○ Make sure you cross reference people in your community and people wanting to connect to ensure they are who you think they are. Also, a different person could be useful for your community as it could be more targeted at what your community offers.

- What you post is a permanent record
  - ○ The best way to fix this is to only post good content and images. Always think before you post about the content and the audience. If it is not right, then do not post it.

- Identity theft exists online
  - ○ The easiest way to prevent this is by having good, strong passwords. Do not have the same passwords across networks, and do not share them with anybody. Make sure that you are present on the main Social Media networks;

that way, if your identity on one is stolen, it will look out of place when people cross reference with your other profiles.

- Emails often have links to viruses, as do posts and links on Social Media
  - As with best practice on emails, do not click on links from Social Media website that you do not know or recognise. The website addresses are normally not spelt correctly or they are just not in the same language as the proper website. If you suspect a virus or spam link, do not click it. Have a look at the website address and contact the person who sent the link.

- People broadcast 'factless facts'; they are often not checked before they are posted and shared
  - Always cross reference and check the authenticity of anything you share. After all, what you share to your network and your community is seen as coming from you and anything that is incorrect will reflect on you and your business.

- People 'buy' likes, views and friends
  - The easy way to see if a profile has fake likes, views etc. is to look at the ratios and history. For example, on a Facebook page that has 1,000 likes, you would expect a few people to like each post, maybe 10 people, but if a profile has say 100,000 likes and each post only receives five likes, it shows that the profile owner has bought the likes and is actually not that credible.

Managing risks on Social Media is not a big issue. It is about managing the risks and understanding the risks. Spend the time getting to understand the privacy and security features on each social network, and ask for advice if you do not understand it.

# Chapter 13: What is the future of Social Media?

## Future of Social Media

Lots of people ask me what the future of Social Media is; what is going to happen with the E-Revolution and the continued growth of Social Media? To be honest, I cannot tell you what is going to happen; I am not psychic and there is no Social Media crystal ball available to me, but what I can tell you is the themes that are emerging and what is going to happen that is going to make things change.

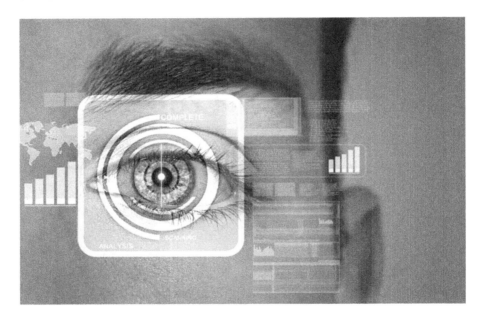

## Mobile, faster and cheaper

The big themes that are happening at the moment are first of all mobile technology and mobile devices. Over the last two or three years, it has been all about mobile and m-commerce (trading via a mobile device). The new world is very much about people buying things, people searching for things, people watching videos, people sharing photos etc. all via mobile devices.

Life with mobile devices is simple. For example, with your smartphone you can take a photo, upload it to a Social Media network and share it with the world, all in a matter of seconds. This allows your community to know where you are, what you are doing, and that you have seen something cool and interesting that you want to share with them.

Another example is finding your way around and using maps on a mobile device. I love Google Maps. When I go to a meeting in London, I know to get from station A to B, but I do not know where to go after that, however with Social Media, it is fine.

I sit on a Tube and chill out, walk out of the station, and open Google maps. I type in the address and follow the directions – that is it. Using a mobile device is a really convenient and efficient way to get around. I do not need to have a map; all I need is my smartphone, although if your phone is out of coverage, you are in trouble!

These are just two simple examples of what you can do on a mobile device. The mobile world is going to get quicker and faster and more interesting. There are two trends that have led to the explosion is mobile devices:

1.  New and faster data networks
2.  New, faster and smaller mobile devices

## New and faster data networks

There are two types of data network that we use for our mobile devices:

1. Mobile phone networks (GPRS, EDGE, 3G, 4G)

2. Data networks (Wi-Fi).

These networks are all improving every day, as the network providers develop faster and cheaper technologies.

Most of us use a mobile device during the day. You start at home with it connected to your own home Wi-Fi network, then on the move you switch to the mobile phone network, and then in the office you connect back into a Wi-Fi network. This wide availability of data networks has allowed us to use the mobile device 24/7 and on the move

In Japan, for example, everybody is on 4G or Wi-Fi and it is significantly faster than anything in the UK. In Japan in five years' time, I am sure you can download the biggest movie ever in 30 seconds and watch it on your phone in HD, and the experience will just be immense.

Over the world, the infrastructure is being upgraded, giving mobile users connections to the Internet wherever and whenever they need it. The more powerful these networks become, the more we will be using the mobile devices and the more rich the experience will become.

## New, faster and smaller mobile devices

The pace of change in the technology, the mobile devices that we use, is continual and relentless. We all hear the news stories when a large technology company launches the next generation of the smartphone, or they launch a new tablet PC. Technology is allowing devices to become smaller and more powerful, allowing us to use more of them on the move with richer content.

We are already seeing watches and glasses which are connected to the Internet. With the glasses, you can walk down the street and see where the nearest restaurants are, take a photo, view your diary and read your emails. With the watch, you can read your emails, make a call and send out some Social Media updates. The technology change will be continual.

The connected home and enabling household appliances with Internet connections is now here. We have Smart TVs that you can use to surf the Internet and connect your photos, but we now have the technology to set your washing machine from your mobile device or adjust your heating when you are on your way home.

The growth of smaller and more powerful devices will change all our lives, not just for years, but for eternity. The development of life will continue whether we like it or not. The technology and the infrastructure is going to grow, which means more data, more downloads and more demand.

## "**Want it now**" demand

We live in a demand-driven world. We live in the world of... I want it now, I want to see it now, I want the music now, I want that product now. The world of on demand is going to grow. We want everything now and we do not want to wait any more.

This new demand-driven behaviour is driven by the relentless development of new technologies and new devices. I remember when I had the Motorola MR1 in the early 1990s, which was one of the first flip phones. I thought that it was the best device I had ever seen and I could not imagine anything better. That lasted a few months and a new device came out that had better features – the MR1 could not send SMS texts, so I needed to upgrade.

This constant world of upgrading is now prevalent across our entire society. We are now pressured from larger companies to get the latest gadgets and eventually the devices we have become obsolete, meaning we have to upgrade again.

A lot of people say to me that they do not take part in this 'latest device world' and they are happy to keep their devices for years, but the reality is that this is not feasible. The large companies are deliberately stopping supporting older devices or not upgrading the software in them, meaning that you have no choice but to be a part of the "want it now" world by default.

The world of "want it now" will continue to grow. The companies behind the E-Revolution invest significant sums of money in development and they only see a return when you and I buy their technology.

I see this is as a world that you need to accept. My advice would be to get the best device you can when you upgrade and keep it for as long as it serves your purpose. This could be six month, or two years. Eventually, the device will become slow, or the software will be unsupported. This is your cue to get a new device and upgrade.

## More choices and more knowledge

The growth of Social Media and technology will give us more choices in life. We have seen over the last few years that Social Media allows us to see and research more than we ever could in the past. This knowledge and research allows us to make better choices, and allows us to make more choices.

The more we know, the more choices we have in life. Social Media will grow our knowledge much further in the future, and we can use this growth in our own knowledge to make better choices in life, as we will understand the options available and the impacts of those.

## "Richer" lives

The future of Social Media will involve more growth and more knowledge, and with knowledge, people will have richer lives. I do not mean people will have more money, I mean that people's knowledge and understanding of the world will be richer and more rounded.

Of course, people may chose not to use Social Media to expand their knowledge, but just using Social Media and joining communities adds more knowledge and richer experience to people.

A richer life will help people make more informed decisions, learn about other people, share knowledge and just be able to connect and support each other in a better way. The world is connecting on Social Media and it is down to your own choice what you learn from those connections and how you can enrich your own life.

### Mobile Payments/Wallets

A very exciting new area for the online world is the ability to pay electronically via Social Media and online services. The world is evolving quickly and transactions are starting to take place where you do not need to share your bank or credit card details. This means transacting online becomes faster and more secure.

As this new technology grows, the ability to transact via Social Media channels will improve.

## Last mile delivery

One of the biggest issues for the future that businesses must solve is how do we bridge the distance from where the products are, to where you want your products to be delivered? In the industry, they call it the 'last mile', and the last mile is probably the biggest issue that any e-business is going to face... How to deliver the product to the customer.

Retailers are trying lots of different solutions, and at the extreme is Amazon who are testing drones. This is a little helicopter that flies into your back garden and drops off your parcel. I am not sure how that will work, but the retailers must try to find a solution that solves this issue.

The more connected and the more mobile we get, the more we can shop whenever and wherever we want, and the bigger this issue will become for the retailers.

A good idea that has been around for a while is 'Click and Collect'. This is where you can order an item and collect it from your local store later that day or the next day. This is a nice service if you are planning to go to the shops later that day or the next day.

Another variation of this is to have your products delivered to a place where you will be walking or driving past later that day or the next day. So far, these have been a shop in your local area, but testing on lockers at train stations and other travel places are currently taking place.

For example, if I want something in the morning, a new jumper, I order it on my mobile device during the day, and on my way home, I go to the station, open a locker and there is the jumper.

This is quick and convenient. This is where we are moving towards with some of the retailers and the locker boxes in terms of in your local High Street, in your local shops, you can order from the big names now and your local newsagents could have your product.

This last mile delivery, where you actually receive your physical product, will see a big change. I am not sure where it is going to end up because it is a physical product, but it will definitely become a quicker and a lot more intuitive for the customers.

## S-Commerce

S-Commerce is a very new part of Social Media:

### *The ability to trade and transact using Social Media.*

At the moment, there is very little opportunity for us to buy anything directly from a Social Media network.

Facebook does have a shopping app that allows a retailer to replicate their shop on Facebook. Twitter is testing a concept with Amazon where you can add a product to your Amazon basket by tweeting.

At the present time, these are all trials and testing of ideas. What I do believe is that S-Commerce will become possible and it will become a large part of people's shopping experience.

Imagine that you are using Facebook and discussing with your community some new products or services. When you are in that conversation, your customers want to buy your product or service. Currently, you would have to send them to another page, for them to register, add to the basket and pay... all taking a lot of time. In the future, your customers will be able to click a button and immediately received the download or receive the confirmation that the product is being delivered.

## The 'dark web' of the Internet

As is common in life, there is good and bad. The Internet is no different, and the world online has developed a whole new darker side where illegal activities and communications take place.

This has been enabled with the use of 'Tor'. Tor is a software application that is used to access the 'Dark Web'. The Tor Project describes their software as "free software and an open network that helps you defend against a form of network surveillance that threatens personal freedom and privacy, confidential business activities and relationships, and state security known as traffic analysis".

This means that you cannot be tracked back to your device or computer, and means you can say and do what you want online without recourse. The world is waking up to this and there will be debates about this for a long time.

For me, it is just a reminder to be careful online and enjoy the world of Social Media and the benefits it will bring to your business and your life.

## Social Media – more networks, more people

Finally, I want to look at the growth of Social Media itself. More people will be connected. For example, Facebook wants to bring the Internet to people less fortunate and in the less-developed countries. They are also trying to bring cheap tablet PCs and cheap laptops so that people in those countries can connect with us and we can connect with them. There is a great value and education that these companies could bring to some of the Third World countries, if they have given them a tablet or a laptop to access the world of data. It is transformational in terms of the standards in the world and education in the world. For me, this is the point of what we are doing in Social Media; we are trying to enrich people in our communities across the world.

Social Media is only going to get bigger. It will get bigger with more networks and more people. As more people get access to the Internet, more people will join the Social Media world.

As we grow into bigger networks, I believe that the world will get more personalised. We will be part of big networks, but within that, we will be part of smaller groups which are specifically your interests. This could be communities with interests in cars, in e-commerce, or in business. We will talk to people around the world; amazing people that want to share your hobby, share your business and share your thoughts.

## Summary

As we come to the end of the book, and the world of Social Media, I want to make sure that you are part of the Social Media world. It is very important that we all grasp the Social Media world; we all need to get on the train and get on the journey now before the train leaves the station.

If you miss the train now, you will struggle to catch up because the world is going to get bigger, and with technology, it is going to get faster and cheaper.

*Remember, with Social Media,*
*you can connect anywhere across the world with anyone*
*and the learning and the power of that,*
*is absolutely immense.*

# Your Social Media journey begins now, and here is my final reminder of what to do:

1. Content, Content, Content
   This is the foundation of Social Media, and the most important asset that you have. In your business, you have lots of content around your products and services. Use this amazing content as more and more content for the Social Media networks. Make your business come to life with online content.

2. Keywords are key
   Finding out your keywords and using them in your content is the key to successful content.  Research your keywords, test them out and use them continuously on your social media.

3. Use the Social Media Strategy
   Write a blog as the basis. Write two paragraphs for Facebook, share on Google + and LinkedIn, write 10 tweets, and share on your networks.

4. Follow people and interact in your communities
   The more you interact and the more content you give, the more people will follow and become engaged with you.

5. Engage and excite
   Once you have a community growing, engage and excite them. Share good content and have great conversations with them. Make them love you!

6. Once you have an engaged community
   Make sure you sell your business and your services! We are in business and we need to make money from our assets.

7. Plan, Plan, Plan
   You must plan your business. Nothing happens without a good plan, hard work and a little bit of luck.  Write your plan NOW and start the journey.

# Chapter 14: Social Media and your business finances

## Does Social Media affect your business finances?

You may think that this is a very strange chapter to include in a book about Social Media, but there is method in my madness.

To start, anything in your business needs to be planned and understood in the context of your entire business. You have limited resources in a business: time, money and people. Working on Social Media will change the business dynamics and finances in a good way!

There are two parts to the Social Media equation:

Social Media Success = Time x Content

The more time you invest and the more targeted your content, the more Social Media success you will gain.

Taking this one step further, if you assume that you already have some time available and you use the principles in this book, you will have a higher success.

As we know, ultimately, the higher the success, the higher the rewards.

## Social Media is free!

The best part of Social Media is the fact it is free! You do not have to pay to use it and interact on it. Using Social Media for your business becomes a no brainer, when you realise that you can use it to market your business at no financial investment.

Of course, you do need time and content. Using the strategies in this book will allow you to maximise the impact and reach of your content, and using the processes will help you reduce the time spent on Social Media.

The biggest time saver is the automated sharing process, which I have covered in a separate chapter.

## Manage your information and finances

As with all parts of your business, you must understand the time you are investing in Social Media as this will take time away from other areas of your business. Managing the time will help you grow your business and you can measure this along with all your other business information.

All businesses have vast amounts of information and data which is very valuable if you manage it and understand it. Using real data that is from trading your business and from your customers can help improve and develop many parts of your business.

In the book, I share the Social Media trackers, these should become part of your management information and be looked at with your other business metrics. Understanding your finances and managing them is key to a successful and profitable business.

Knowing where your money comes from and goes to is something you should understand on a regular basis – even daily for sales and cash.

Remember: you must manage cash correctly – cash is king, and without cash, your business will fail.

# Know and understand your profit and loss account

Your profit and loss account (P&L) is the place to find out where your money comes from and where it goes to.

It starts with the money coming in (sales revenue), and it takes off the cost of those sales (cost of goods sold) to give you the profit from your product buying (gross profit).

Gross profit = sales revenue - costs of goods sold

Once you have your gross profit, divide by the sales to get a gross margin percent.

Gross profit margin = (gross profit ÷ sales revenue) x 100

**Example: calculating gross profit margin**

Below is an example profit margin for a bakery that sells cakes, pastries, pasties, pies and a variety of bread loaves.

| Product | Cost of Goods (£) | Sale price (£) Inc VAT | Gross profit (£) | Gross profit margin (%) |
|---|---|---|---|---|
| **Tiger Loaf** | 0.50 | 2.00 | 1.50 | 75% |
| **Chocolate Croissant** | 1.00 | 3.00 | 2.00 | 66% |
| **Sausage Roll** | 1.50 | 2.00 | 0.50 | 25% |

If the bakery sold 180 chocolate croissants, 106 tiger loaves and 100 sausage rolls a day, the gross profits would be:

| Product | Daily target | Gross profit (£) | Gross profit margin | Daily gross profit (£) |
|---|---|---|---|---|
| Tiger Loaf | 106 | 1.50 | 75% | 159 |
| Chocolate Croissant | 180 | 2.00 | 66% | 360 |
| Sausage Roll | 100 | 0.50 | 25% | 50 |
| Totals | 386 | | | 569 |

As a business owner, this is a useful exercise to understand what your most profitable and unprofitable products lines are. You may even decide to stop offering some unprofitable lines and concentrate on your most profitable products.

Once you have your gross profit, take off all your other costs and you are left with your profit (or loss).

Your other costs will be all the costs of your business:

- Salaries
- Rent
- Rates
- Marketing
- Advertising
- Office equipment
- Stationery
- Travel
- Accountant
- Merchant services
- Bank charges
- Taxes

P&Ls should be reviewed on a weekly or monthly basis. In the beginning, managing your P&L daily is important to make sure you know where you are spending your cash.

Understanding the P&L allows you to make business decisions based on real facts within your business. Over time, you will need to make positive and negative decisions, and these will all have an effect on the P&L; understanding that impact before you make a decision is very important.

The easiest way to get to know your P&L is by looking at it regularly, starting with sales which you can review every day.

1. Review your sales data daily
2. Learn what is selling and what is not
3. Understand your product margins
4. Check your bank account weekly
5. Understand your costs

## Plan, Forecast, Budget

Throughout the book, I have stressed the need to plan and forecast your business. Social Media is just one part of your overall business plan and it is important to start planning what the costs and revenue impacts are to your business.

Once you have an understanding of your products and services, your business plan and an understanding of your marketing and sales plan, you can then put together a budget or forecast that predicts what you plan to sell each week and what the cost of those sales will be.

With all the plans together, you will then be able to forecast the costs within the business. These can then be measured to ensure you are on track and the business is performing as you wish it to.

A basic P&L format (this can be Budget, Forecast or Actual) is below.

| Budget/Forecast/ Actual | Period 1 | Period 2 | Period 3 |
|---|---|---|---|
| **Sales Revenue** | | | |
| Cost of Goods | | | |
| **Gross Margin** | | | |
| Costs: | | | |
| Staff | | | |
| Office Rent/Rates | | | |
| Marketing/Advertising | | | |
| Store Overheads | | | |
| Delivery/Logistics | | | |
| Finance/Admin | | | |
| **Profit before Tax** | | | |

This format can be used for different periods (i.e. weeks, months, years) and different types (i.e. Actual, Budget, Forecast). All formats should remain consistent and all items should be calculated in the same way; this will enable comparisons and trends to be analysed.

## Cash is King

The management of cash will make or break a business – businesses fail due to lack of cash, not lack of profits. Therefore, managing the cash and the bank account is extremely important.

> The retail industry is a great 'cash' industry that most industries would be jealous of, due to its ability to manage to a positive cash flow situation.
>
> This means that retailers (in certain sectors) can retail products that are bought by the customer before you have paid the supplier – this is called positive cash flow, as you will have the money in the bank from the customer before you pay for the products you have just sold.
>
> Since the financial crisis, this has been much harder to achieve, but striving to achieve a positive cash flow is a great target.

The way to manage to a positive cash flow situation is to set up your suppliers' payment terms for a longer period than you need to sell the item.

For example, if you negotiate payment terms of 60 days with your supplier and you sell the product to your customer for cash on day 30, you will have 30 days left before you pay your supplier.

Whichever method you use to manage your supplier relationships and customer relationships, you need to manage cash on a daily basis.

A simple reconciliation each day of your sales revenues and your costs can easily ensure you know where you are with your finances.

An example cash flow statement:

| Budget/Forecast/ Actual | Period 1 | Period 2 | Period 3 |
|---|---|---|---|
| **Balance Brought Forward** | **£5,000** | **£10,000** | **£8,000** |
| **Sales Revenue (Cleared)** | **£10,000** | **£10,000** | **£10,000** |
| Cost of Goods | | £10,000 | |
| Costs: | | | |
| Staff | | £2,000 | |
| Office Rent/Rates | £5,000 | | |
| Marketing/Advertising | | | £5,000 |
| Store Overheads | | | |
| Delivery/Logistics | | | £2,000 |
| Finance/Admin | | | |
| **Balance Carried Forward** | **£10,000** | **£8,000** | **£11,000** |

In this example cash flow, we started the period with £5,000 in cash in the bank and made cash sales of £10,000. We then paid the rent and ended the period at £10,000 cash in the bank. This was then rolled forward to the next period and we then spent £2,000 on staff expenses leaving £8,000 in the bank.

As you can see, this simple model will ensure you can monitor and manage your cash. At the end of any period, you should be able to reconcile the balance carried forward figure easily to your bank balance and any borrowings you may have.

Planning your cash flow from day one will help you understand your peaks and troughs with regard to cash.

Most retailers have seasonal peaks and, in the main, this happens at Christmas. Managing cash during the quiet periods could be challenging, as there will be times of the year when sales are very low, but you still have to pay monthly bills etc.

Planning this in advance will allow you to approach your bank and ask for a flexible loan or an overdraft. Most retailers will use flexible financing through the quieter sales periods.

## Analyse your information

Analysis is best described as 'making sense of information and data'.

In your business, you will have a lot of information and data, and all this data is useful to you and your business. As long as you can understand what the data is telling you, you will be able to act on this information.

Analysis needs to be simple and customer-focused. You are looking for trends and information that will improve your business, which means the improvements you need to make to enable your customer to be satisfied.

The main analysis any business should look at will be the sales and the margins. You need to understand what this is telling you: where you are selling products, what products are selling and what products are not selling. You also need to understand what products are making you a good margin and what are making poor margins, and act on this analysis.

A list of the main areas to analyse is below (this is just a start; in your business, there will be many more things that you can analyse to help improve your business):

- Sales
  - What products are selling
  - What products are not selling
  - How many products are selling
  - What customer segments are buying
  - Which channels are products selling in
  - What times of the day, and which days, do products sell

- Margins
  - What each product margin is
  - How much you are marking down/discounting products
  - Which customer segments are better margin contributors

- Social Media
  - Which channel is driving the most visitors to the website
  - What products are the customers discussing the most
  - Which videos are being shared the most
  - What times of day are the most interactive posts

- Costs
  - Staffing
  - Logistics and Delivery
  - Marketing
  - Promotions
  - Overheads

For Social Media, understanding whether your customers click through to your website is a key measure. If you can see that you have website visitors from Facebook or Twitter, you know the Social Media channels are working. They are driving customers to your website and this is what you want to see.

Analysis of all these areas will help to identify trends and these are important for decision making.

For example, if you analyse sales by customer segment, you may find that one segment is continually buying lower margin products. You can then investigate why this is happening and work out a strategy to convert these customers to higher margin products.

Once you have identified a trend, and you have investigated the reasons for that trend, you must act and develop a strategy to improve or develop this trend.

Ongoing analysis and building up an understanding of the trends and drivers within your business will help you buy better products, reduce costs and make a healthy profit.

Lots of information and analysis is great, but you need to act on this information and make sure you put plans in place to achieve the improvements desired.

Many businesses make the mistake of not acting on the analysis and end up in a worse situation because of this. Make sure you make a decision and change things based on the analysis.

Would you like to know more?
Would you like to connect with your fellow
community on Social Media?

Please join our two groups for
Social Media Essentials, where you will get the
latest advice, models and support.

You can interact with all your community as well as
author Antony Welfare.

 https://www.linkedin.com/groups/
Social-Media-Essentials-3887706

 https://www.facebook.com/
SocialMediaEssential

Enjoy your Social Media journey!

Lightning Source UK Ltd.
Milton Keynes UK
UKOW06f0601161015

260685UK00001B/20/P

9 781910 125861